GREAT AMERICAN THINKERS

Thurgood Marshall

The First African-American Supreme Court Justice

Rebecca Carey Rohan

Cavendish Square

New York

Published in 2017 by Cavendish Square Publishing, LLC
243 5th Avenue, Suite 136, New York, NY 10016

Copyright © 2017 by Cavendish Square Publishing, LLC

First Edition

Website: cavendishsq.com

This publication represents the opinions and views of the author based on his or her
personal experience, knowledge, and research. The information in this book serves as a general
guide only. The author and publisher have used their best efforts in preparing this book and
disclaim liability rising directly or indirectly from the use and application of this book.

CPSIA Compliance Information: CS16CSQ

All websites were available and accurate when this book was sent to press.

Library of Congress Cataloging-in-Publication Data

Names: Rohan, Rebecca Carey, 1967- author. Title: Thurgood Marshall :
the first African-American Supreme Court justice / Rebecca Rohan.
Description: New York : Cavendish Square Publishing, 2017. |
Series: Great American thinkers | Includes bibliographical references and index.
Identifiers: LCCN 2016003473 (print) | LCCN 2016005301 (ebook) |
ISBN 9781502619327 (library bound) | ISBN 9781502619334 (ebook)
Subjects: LCSH: Marshall, Thurgood, 1908-1993--Juvenile literature. | United
States. Supreme Court--Biography--Juvenile literature. | African America judges--
Biography--Juvenile literature. | African American lawyers--Biography--Juvenile literature.
Classification: LCC KF8745.M34 R64 2016 (print) | LCC KF8745.M34 (ebook) |
DDC 347.73/2634--dc23
LC record available at http://lccn.loc.gov/2016003473

Editorial Director: David McNamara
Editor: Elizabeth Schmermund
Copy Editor: Nathan Heidelberger
Art Director: Jeffrey Talbot
Designer: Amy Greenan
Production Assistant: Karol Szymczuk
Photo Research: J8 Media

The photographs in this book are used by permission and through the courtesy of: Bachrach/Archive
Photos/Getty Images, cover; Russell Lee/Library of Congress, 4; Gene Forte/Consolidated News Pictures/
Archive Photos/Getty Images, 7; Keystone Press Agency/Keystone USA/ZUMAPRESS.com, 9, 27;
Library of Congress, 11, 111; William Lovelace/Express/Hulton Archive/Getty Images, 13; AP Images,
17, 49, 54, 84; Everett Collection/Newscom, 18; Yoichi Okamoto/LBJ Library, 22; William P. Gottlieb/
Library of Congress, 34 left; Carl Van Vechten/Library of Congress, 34 right; Afro American Newspapers/
Gado/Archive Photos/Getty Images, 36; Ed Clark/The LIFE Picture Collection/Getty Images, 39; Everett
Collection Historical/Alamy Stock Photo, 41, 60-61, 68-69; Paul Richards/AFP/Getty Images, 43; NAACP/
Library of Congress, 44; Ralph Morse/The LIFE Picture Collection/Getty Images, 51; Carl Iwasaki/
The LIFE Picture Collection/Getty Images, 58; Thomas J. O'Halloran/Library of Congress, 78; Warren
K. Leffler/Library of Congress, 83; U.S. Army, 88-89; Marion S. Trikosko/Library of Congress, 91; Steve
Liss/The LIFE Picture Collection/Getty Images, 96; National Archives and Records Administration,
99; Steve Petteway/Supreme Court of the United States, 105; Paul Marotta/Getty Images, 100.

Printed in the United States of America

CONTENTS

INTRODUCTION ... 5
Two Turning Points in the History of Racism in America

ONE ... 9
A Life Lived Before and After

TWO ... 27
His Life and Times

THREE ... 45
His Contemporaries

FOUR ... 59
A Professional Life in Pursuit of a Singular Goal

FIVE ... 79
Life Goes On

SIX ... 97
Brown v. Board of Education Today

Chronology / 112

Glossary / 114

Sources / 117

Further Information / 122

Bibliography / 124

Index / 125

About the Author / 128

INTRODUCTION

Two Turning Points in the History of Racism in America

For more than 175 years, from its establishment in 1789 until 1967, every single judge appointed to serve on the Supreme Court of the United States was a white man. There were no men of color, and certainly no women of any race. This was especially problematic because the main job of the Supreme Court is to uphold the laws of the country, especially the highest law of all: the US Constitution.

The Constitution is the document that defines and defends the basic rights of United States citizens—but not all citizens were being represented on the Supreme Court. During this time, white men handled every court challenge, in a country that considered black people to be second-class citizens.

An African-American man drinks from the "colored" water cooler at a streetcar station in Oklahoma City, Oklahoma, in the mid-1950s.

Before 1865, slavery was legal. It was abolished after the Civil War through the passing of the Thirteenth Amendment to the Constitution, but the people of the United States hadn't yet figured out how to accommodate this change. Many white people were too used to assuming that black people were an inferior race, even if they were no longer slaves.

States felt free to pass laws saying that white people and black people didn't have to share public facilities or live in the same neighborhoods. They prevented black people from voting or owning property and placed many other restrictions on their lives. Schools for black children, if they existed, were blatantly insufficient.

The term "**Jim Crow laws**" is often used to describe the actions that states, many of them in the South, took against African Americans between 1877 and the mid-1960s. But there was more to this mindset than laws. Scholars now say there was a "Jim Crow **etiquette**" that pervaded the lives of black citizens. Both the laws and American society were based on the following beliefs: Whites were superior to blacks in all important ways; sexual relations between blacks and whites would produce a **mongrel** race that would destroy America; and treating blacks as equals or socializing with them would encourage such unions. Worst of all, people believed that it was alright to use violence to keep blacks at the bottom of the racial hierarchy.

The first time the all-white-male Supreme Court had to consider the state of racism in the country was in 1896. In 1892, an African-American train passenger named Homer Plessy refused to sit in a "colored only" car, breaking a Louisiana Jim Crow law. Plessy went to court claiming that his constitutional rights had been violated, but after he lost his case at the state level, the Supreme Court upheld the lower court's decision. The court ruled that segregation was constitutional under the "separate but equal" doctrine. Restrictive legislation based on race continued until the case called *Brown v. Board of Education of Topeka, Kansas* in 1954. This historical court case would, for the first time in United States history, challenge the entrenched Jim Crow laws and pave the way for a more just society.

The justices of the Supreme Court of the United States in October 1970. Thurgood Marshall is on the far left in the back row.

The attorney who argued this important case was none other than Thurgood Marshall, a highly educated, accomplished attorney who had already successfully argued twenty-eight cases in front of the Supreme Court. He was also African American, and the grandson of a slave. Thirteen years later, in 1967, President Lyndon B. Johnson appointed Thurgood Marshall to the Supreme Court. He became the first African American to ever serve on the court, and he did so for twenty-four years. Thurgood Marshall's life story shows the incredible progress that took place during this period in US history, despite the many challenges he faced due to the color of his skin. What brought Thurgood Marshall to that moment in history? How did it impact the country from then until now? Knowing Marshall's life story, and understanding the America in which he grew up, will help to answer these questions.

CHAPTER ONE

A Life Lived Before and After

The years during which Thurgood Marshall grew to adulthood had a definite and obvious influence on the man he would become. Beyond the influences of his family and the middle-class community in which they lived, the country was in turmoil for decades over the matters of race and equality. As he grew older and learned about the injustices that were occurring in the United States, Marshall realized he wanted to do something about them. He devoted most of his life to ending segregation and fighting for equality.

The Early 1900s

Thurgood Marshall, named Thoroughgood Marshall at birth, was born barely forty years after slavery was abolished in 1865. In fact, although all four of his grandparents had been born in the United States, his paternal grandfather, the

Marshall poses for a professional portrait during his years as a circuit court judge.

original Thorough Good Marshall, had been a slave. His maternal grandfather, who ran a grocery store in Baltimore, tried to mobilize the black community against police brutality as early as 1875. He also spoke out against the Ku Klux Klan, an all-white group that hid under hoods and robes to terrorize and kill black people, especially in the South.

Thurgood was born in 1908, in Baltimore, Maryland, a state that is technically in the South due to its location below the Mason-Dixon Line. The Mason-Dixon Line is the name given to the border between Pennsylvania and Maryland. It is named after two British astronomers, Charles Mason and Jeremiah Dixon, who were charged with determining exactly where the border between the states lay. Leaders of the two states at the time wanted the boundary defined due to ownership—but the line's true significance is that it separates the states that did not permit slavery before the Civil War from those that did.

Even in the North, which had not had laws permitting slavery, violence and prejudice against African Americans was widespread. The same year as Marshall's birth, eighty-nine African Americans were **lynched** across the United States, most likely for crimes they did not commit, or for crimes that did not merit such violent retaliation. In Springfield, Illinois, a race war broke out between white and black residents. A white mob tried to break into the jail and kill two black men who were suspected of crimes against white people. After weeks of riots, looting, and killing, the battles finally ended. Six people were dead and dozens more were injured, and more than forty black families were displaced when their houses were destroyed. Sadly, anti-black race riots in northern cities were nothing new in the early twentieth century.

At the time Marshall was born, the United States was still living under the "separate but equal" doctrine. Back in 1896, a man named Homer Plessy sued the state of Louisiana, saying that the state's law requiring him to sit in a "colored" car on the train violated his

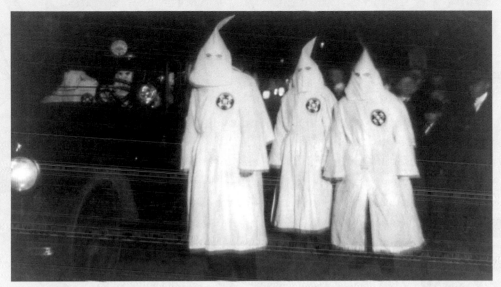

The Ku Klux Klan paraded openly through the streets during their reign of terror.

THE KU KLUX KLAN IN AMERICA

The Ku Klux Klan (KKK), America's longest-running hate group, was founded in 1866 in Tennessee. The KKK was formed after the Civil War, in reaction to those people who supported equal rights for African Americans. All members of this vigilante group were white, and they hid their identities under white robes and hoods with small eyeholes. They were famous for their night rides where they attacked, terrorized, and sometimes killed black men, usually for the "crime" of attempting to exercise their civil rights, like voting. They carried out lynchings, tar-and-featherings, rapes, and other violent attacks on anyone who challenged white supremacy. Although the first members dialed down their activities after Jim Crow laws went into effect, they came back in full force in the 1960s, during the height of the civil rights movement.

rights under the US Constitution. An early civil rights organization took his case all the way to the Supreme Court—and as unbelievable as this sounds now, the court backed the state of Louisiana. In the famous *Plessy v. Ferguson* decision, the judges said that separate facilities for blacks and whites were constitutional as long as they were equal. Unfortunately, the people in power applied the "separate but equal" policy to many areas of public life, including restaurants, theaters, restrooms, and schools.

There were plenty of Jim Crow laws on the books that enforced racial segregation, especially in the South. White people and black people couldn't eat in the same restaurants, sit in the same sections at movie theaters, or go to the same schools. There were separate entrances for people of color at banks and other public buildings. When riding on trolley cars, whites were allowed to board before blacks, who then had to ride in the back. Even cemeteries were segregated! Worst of all, in many states, African Americans couldn't vote, own property, or run for office. This was the world in which Thurgood Marshall grew up.

The Great Migration

From around the time Marshall started school until 1920, especially in the years following the end of World War I, roughly five hundred thousand African-American Southerners moved to the large cities of the North, like Chicago, New York, Cleveland, Pittsburgh, and Detroit. They wanted to escape the oppression and poverty they faced in the South, where they were being stripped of their rights, such as the ability to vote, and being denied equal protection under the law. While this was an important period for the African-American community (the **Harlem Renaissance** was launched during this era, for example), racial tensions escalated in some of these cities. In 1919, a riot broke out in Chicago after police refused to arrest a white boy for throwing rocks at a black boy who swam in the "whites only" section of Lake Michigan,

In 1961, in Jackson, Mississippi, the police were expected to enforce segregated waiting rooms.

causing him to drown. People rioted for five days, and thirty-eight people lost their lives. Much closer to Marshall's home, just 40 miles (64 kilometers) south in Washington, DC, another race riot occurred that same year between white and black war veterans. After three nights of fighting, federal troops brought an end to the violence. Marshall heard about this incident and was shocked at how even veterans of color weren't safe from racism.

The 1930s

By the 1930s, the National Association for the Advancement of Colored People (NAACP), a civil rights organization founded in 1909, intensified its work to desegregate schools. Thurgood Marshall experienced this prejudice in regard to his education himself—upon graduating from college, he wanted to attend law school at the University of Maryland but was turned down there due to the color of his skin.

In 1932, the NAACP received a grant that would allow the group to fight against the segregation of schools in the South. This project would be led by a man named Charles Hamilton Houston, who was the dean at the Howard University School of Law, where Marshall studied, and who became Marshall's **mentor**. Marshall himself would accompany Houston to the Deep South to see the conditions of the schools for themselves. They were horrified at the deplorable condition of the school buildings, the lack of teaching materials, and the poverty of the children. This was one of the experiences that inspired Marshall to make the world a better place for his people, and he grew even more convinced that he could do this best by being a lawyer.

However, being an African-American attorney was not easy in those days. White firms wouldn't hire black lawyers. Many worked alone for that reason, but even black people wouldn't hire them because they knew the law community was prejudiced against them. After graduating from law school, Marshall set up his own office and tried to find clients. At first, things didn't go so well for Marshall's career. For one of his very first cases, he had to defend himself in court! This was because he encouraged the black community in Baltimore not to shop at a chain of stores that refused to hire African Americans. When the owners found out that Marshall was behind the **boycott**, they took legal action against him, but in the end, Marshall won. The judge in the case agreed with Marshall's argument that people could shop wherever they wanted, and if they didn't want to shop at stores that wouldn't hire certain people, they had that right. During this time, Marshall also forced the desegregation of a number of Baltimore golf clubs.

When he had downtime due to lack of clients, Marshall continued to accompany Charles Houston on trips to the Deep South on missions for the NAACP. In 1936, Houston asked Marshall to run the NAACP's New York office. While there, he took on the problem of inequality in teachers' salaries. He discovered that many school systems paid their white and African-American teachers different salaries. Sometimes, the black teachers made only half of what their white counterparts made. He found an African-American school principal named Walter Mills who was suing his local school board for the same reason and took on his case.

In order to gather evidence for *Mills v. Board of Education of Anne Arundel County*, Marshall found a school superintendent in Maryland who publicly said that "the worst white teacher was better than the best black teacher." Then he found a school principal who would challenge that statement in court. When the case was over in 1939, the judge agreed with Marshall, and the state of Maryland realized that they had better pass a law guaranteeing a standard pay scale for all teachers, regardless of their race, or they'd be facing years of expensive lawsuits. As Marshall pursued and won similar cases in other states, those states came to the same realization.

These cases were important victories for African Americans in the teaching profession; however, nationwide, racial discrimination still ruled. Especially in the South, it was still common to see signs that said "For White Customers Only" or "Colored Citizens Use the Back Door" or those indicating which water fountains or restrooms could be used by which race. If blacks violated these restrictions, they faced serious trouble.

The 1940s

World War II was a turning point for African Americans in the United States. During the four years of US involvement in the war, many enlisted to fight for their country. They were invited to join the ranks of the marines for the first time ever. The army appointed its first black brigadier general, Benjamin O. Davis Sr. One person who noticed the contributions of the black community to the American cause was President Harry S. Truman. In 1948, he proclaimed that if African Americans were willing to fight and die for their country, they should be treated equally. He banned discrimination both in the military and in all government jobs. He even set up a study, with the research to be performed by both whites and blacks, to examine the problem of race discrimination in the United States.

The 1950s

Even with the support of a president, racism and segregation still existed. Thurgood Marshall won his greatest, most famous case, *Brown v. Board of Education of Topeka, Kansas*, in 1954. It abolished school segregation in the United States and offered a foundation for African Americans to fight segregation in other areas of life. But, in the late 1950s, a movement called **massive resistance** began. Many people did not want to comply with anti-segregation laws in schools or elsewhere, especially in the Deep South. Racists often threw bricks through the windows of black families' homes; the bricks were often wrapped in notes threatening them with further harm if they sent their children to white schools. The children themselves were spit on and hit. Many black parents lost their jobs, and white people

Marshall and fellow attorneys George E. C. Hayes and James M. Nabrit pose outside the Supreme Court on May 17, 1954, the day they won the *Brown v. Board of Education* case.

Marshall confers with fellow attorneys Harold Boulware and Spottswood Robinson during the argument phase of the *Brown v. Board of Education* case.

boycotted stores run by black people. Worst of all, some schools still refused to honor desegregation.

In one famous incident, nine African-American students were supposed to start the school year at Central High School in Little Rock, Arkansas, on September 3, 1957. When they tried to enter the school, they were met by a vicious mob of white students, parents, and citizens screaming at them and attempting to keep them off the school grounds. To make matters worse, the governor **intervened**, but instead of helping the children, he ordered the Arkansas National Guard to prevent them from entering the building. Nearly three weeks later, a federal judge ordered the governor to remove the National Guard from Central High School's entrance, and he defied the court order. President Dwight Eisenhower had to step in. He sent nearly one thousand 101st Airborne Division paratroopers to Little Rock, put the Arkansas National Guard under federal command, and ordered them all to protect the "Little Rock Nine," as the students came to be known, as they entered the school. The army guarded the school for the rest of the year in order to ensure that there was no further trouble.

Arkansas's governor was not the only one who tried to ignore *Brown v. Board of Education of Topeka, Kansas*. Others said they did not want to obey the law because they feared it was not in the best interest of African-American students—especially in terms of their welfare and safety—to be forced to go to school with white children. Thurgood Marshall went back to the Supreme Court for assistance, and in 1958, the court **unanimously** decreed that Supreme Court law could not be ignored on the state level. Governors could not pick and choose which federal laws to follow.

The 1960s

The 1960s is the decade perhaps most associated with the rise of the civil rights movement and the corresponding collapse of lawful segregation. From the get-go, the 1960s were a time when black people started making headway in publicizing their causes. In February 1960, four black college students sat down at a "whites only" Woolworth's lunch counter in Greensboro, North Carolina. They were refused service, but they would not leave their seats. More students volunteered to continue the sit-in, and as word spread, similar protests took place on other college campuses in more than sixty-five cities in twelve states. Thousands of young African Americans participated in protests in that year alone, including swim-ins at segregated swimming pools and pray-ins at white-only churches.

Leaders such as Martin Luther King Jr. and Malcolm X rose to prominence. King, a former Baptist minister, was an especially influential man. He was a passionate, engaging speaker, and he preached "peaceful resistance," or nonviolent action—but he definitely preached that taking immediate action was the way to go. He wasn't against people breaking the law if it got the message across; for example, he encouraged sit-ins. This was in direct contrast to Thurgood Marshall, who wanted to accomplish equal rights not by breaking the laws but by changing them. The two men did work together sometimes, however. The legal arm of the NAACP, the Legal Defense and Educational Fund, which Marshall had helped establish, actually defended Dr. King more than once, including in the case that arose from the Montgomery bus boycott that he organized in 1955.

Marshall also disagreed strongly with Malcolm X and the Nation of Islam's calls for African-American separatism. They wanted to establish a black nation and therefore supported the idea that blacks and whites should be separate. After everything Marshall had done to bring the two races together, he couldn't support such ideals. In fact, the Nation of Islam once threatened him, saying he was too chummy with white people. Marshall's was a different kind of civil rights activism: he wasn't marching and shouting in the streets; he was making his voice heard and his presence known in the courtrooms. By this time, though, people found it easier to relate to Dr. King and others like him, who seemed to be taking a more active stance than Thurgood Marshall.

The civil rights movement had an **ally** in the new president, John F. Kennedy. He and his brother Robert F. Kennedy had already shown support for Martin Luther King Jr. when King was arrested shortly before Kennedy's election. As president, Kennedy selected record numbers of African Americans to fill high-level positions in his administration. He also strengthened the Civil Rights Commission and put his vice president, Lyndon B. Johnson, in charge of the President's Committee on Equal Employment Opportunity. Most importantly, he appointed Thurgood Marshall to be a federal judge of the Second Circuit Court of Appeals in New York. This meant that Marshall would be responsible for deciding which cases in the states of New York, Vermont, and Connecticut would be heard by the Supreme Court.

Needless to say, this was a huge step forward for not only Thurgood Marshall but for the civil rights of African Americans. There were very few black judges in the United States at the time, and in such a high-ranking position, Marshall wielded a lot of power. He always ruled fairly, and during his time on the job, none of his decisions were turned over by a higher court.

President Kennedy's successor, Lyndon Johnson, took over the presidency after Kennedy's assassination. President Johnson was a liberal Democrat who strongly supported civil rights and knew how to work with Congress to get laws passed. His most significant achievement was the passage of the Civil Rights Act of 1964, which has been defined as "without question, the most powerful package of civil rights laws in the history of the nation." The Civil Rights Act outlaws discrimination in the workplace, in public spaces such as hotels and restaurants, and in voting booths during elections. Johnson knew he would need strong support from the other branches of the government to enforce this act, and one of the first steps he took in office was to offer the role of solicitor general of the United States to Thurgood Marshall.

As the media crowd around, President Lyndon B. Johnson (*seated in wheelchair*) announces his decision to nominate Thurgood Marshall (*seated center*) as the first African-American Supreme Court justice.

The job of the solicitor general of the United States is to argue cases before the Supreme Court—which Marshall had already done successfully, twenty-eight times—but on behalf of the government. In other words, Marshall would be one of the most powerful lawyers in the nation, but he'd be arguing from the other side of the courtroom, figuratively speaking. He would also have regular access to the president and the chance to influence the country's laws directly.

Marshall accepted the job, and he became the first African American ever to hold the position. He brought many cases before the Supreme Court, and he won almost all of them. In one, he argued that the state of Mississippi was not doing enough to prosecute the murderers of three young civil rights workers—two of whom were white—who were shot on a back road in Mississippi while working to register African Americans to vote in upcoming elections. He convinced the justices that these were not just murders, but "acts of racial terrorism that violated federal laws." The Supreme Court agreed. The killers were tried in federal court and sent to jail. Another of Marshall's most important cases was related to voting, too. After President Johnson passed the Voting Rights Act of 1965, which said that all US citizens, regardless of race, had the right to vote in any election, some states tried to get around allowing black people to vote. They stated that voters had to pay a fee, called a poll tax, in order to participate, knowing that many minorities would not be able to afford it. When a court in Virginia shot down a challenge to the state's poll tax, Marshall brought the case to the Supreme Court. The nine justices unanimously agreed with Marshall that the practice was unfair, and Virginia had to abolish the poll tax.

National Turbulence

Civil rights was not the only issue dividing the nation in the late 1960s. The United States had entered the Vietnam War, helping South Vietnam fight North Vietnam's attempt to take over the southern part of the country. Many American citizens thought that America should not have gotten involved. They didn't like that the United States was spending billions of dollars on the war, but mostly, they were upset and angry over the more than fifty thousand US soldiers who were killed in action.

People were also beginning to turn against President Johnson, who had promised to wage a war on poverty. He had wanted to create "The Great Society," where everybody was treated the same, regardless of race, and had equal access to food, clothing, and shelter. He implemented programs aimed at closing the gap between rich and poor, and he passed the American Opportunity Act, which included such programs as Upward Bound and Head Start that are still part of the American educational system today. He also tried to empower local action initiatives, or Community Action Programs (CAPs), to combat poverty in individual communities, and placed local black leaders in charge. However, this policy sometimes caused backlash from local white politicians and law enforcement. Black people were subject to uniformed brutality, which often went unpunished. Especially in the inner cities, the people were angry and fed up. They started riots, where property was damaged and other people were killed or seriously hurt.

In the midst of all this turmoil, however, President Johnson made a significant decision. He knew that one of the Supreme Court's justices, Tom Clark, had plans to retire in 1967. It was Johnson's job to appoint a new justice, although his decision would have to be approved by the United States Senate. He considered a few candidates, including a woman, but in the end, President Johnson asked Thurgood Marshall to take the position. Marshall said yes. He passed a days-long **grilling** by the Senate, and on October 2, 1967, Thurgood Marshall became the first African-American judge to hold a position on the Supreme Court of the United States of America.

The 1970s

As a justice of the Supreme Court, Thurgood Marshall had to hear, and vote on, many cases that did not involve racial discrimination. He supported the rights of the homeless, the mentally ill, and women. One of the most famous cases he voted on in this decade was *Roe v. Wade*, which legalized abortion. He also championed a movement called **affirmative action**.

Affirmative action programs were introduced in 1963 under President Kennedy. They were designed to help end discrimination against minority groups, including African Americans, other people of color, and women of all races. The idea was that such programs could improve employment or educational opportunities for people who had been discriminated against for decades. Affirmative action policies, programs, and procedures were designed to give preference to minorities and women in job hiring, college admissions, the awarding of government contracts, and other areas where they had typically been shut out.

However, by the late 1970s, people started to challenge court decisions made in favor of affirmative action. They claimed that such policies were a form of "reverse discrimination." The Supreme Court heard the first major challenge in 1978, in a case called *Regents of the University of California v. Bakke*. They ruled, with a slim majority, that quotas should not reserve spots for minority applicants if whites were barred from applying for those same spots. Similar cases continued to crop up well into the 1990s.

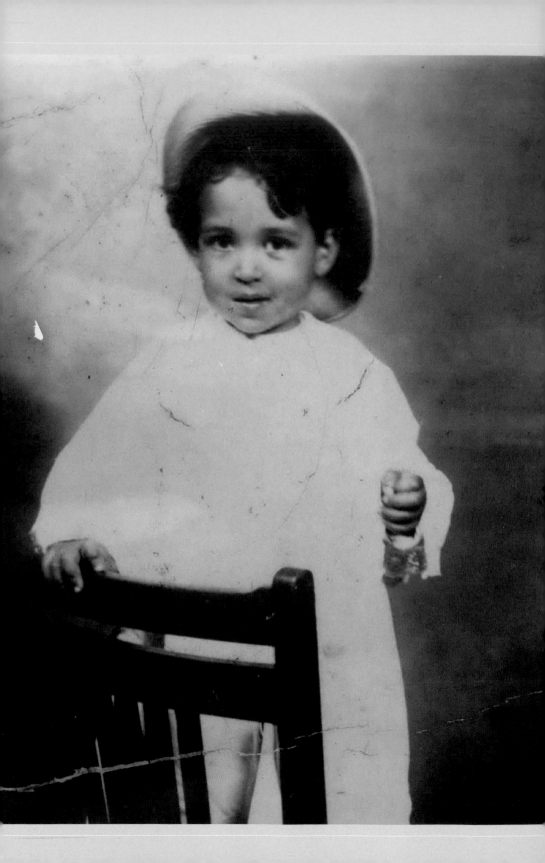

CHAPTER TWO

⌒

His Life and Times

When looking at pictures of an adult Thurgood Marshall, it's hard to imagine that he was once a little boy. In most pictures from his professional life, he is dressed formally, and he is rarely shown smiling. He looks serious, studious, and every inch a respected judge. Yet, from all accounts, he was a bright, talkative, and argumentative child with a bit of a mischievous streak. While nobody could have predicted that he would become the first African-American Supreme Court justice, the aspects of his personality that made him such a successful lawyer and judge seem to have been part of him all along.

Two-year-old Thurgood Marshall

Early Life and Family

Thoroughgood Marshall, as he was named when he was born on July 2, 1908, was the second-born son of a comfortably middle-class family in Baltimore, Maryland. His father, Willie, worked for the Baltimore and Ohio Railroad (better known as the B&O Railroad) as a dining-car waiter. Willie made a decent living, but he always felt that his lack of higher education held him back. He impressed upon Thoroughgood and his older brother, Aubrey, the importance of going to college.

Norma Williams Marshall, their mother, went so far as to say that she hoped Aubrey would be a doctor and his younger brother would be a dentist. She probably couldn't imagine what her younger son would eventually become! Aubrey did eventually study medicine and dentistry, and he became a doctor.

The Williams family was **cultured**; Norma was named after an opera, while her sister and brother were named after characters from Shakespeare. This was due to their father, Isaiah Williams, who had traveled the world with the navy, developed a taste for the theater and classical music, and then returned to Baltimore to run a thriving grocery business.

Isaiah Williams was also an outspoken member of the Baltimore business community who didn't like the way black people were treated in the city. As early as 1875, he tried to organize meetings to protest against white-on-black police brutality and the Ku Klux Klan's attempts to take over Maryland politics. It's safe to assume that his grandsons picked up at least some of his opinions about race discrimination in Baltimore, as well as his outspokenness.

Thoroughgood was named after his paternal grandfather, who originally spelled the name as two words: Thorough Good. The younger Thoroughgood altered the name again as a **precocious** second grader. He announced that Thoroughgood took too long to write, so he was going to shorten his name to Thurgood. He even asked his mother to have his birth certificate altered to reflect the change.

Thorough Good Marshall was a former slave who fought in the Civil War. His father (Thurgood's great-grandfather) was also a slave, and the family proudly tells a legendary story about him: They claim that he was brought to America from the Congo to serve as a slave, but that he was so stubborn and insubordinate that his owner freed him.

Thurgood's grandfather also owned a grocery store, and his grandmother Annie Marshall helped him run it. The family's favorite story about Annie was her refusal to let the Baltimore Gas and Electric Company install a streetlight right in front of the store. She felt it would spoil her view, so she told the company they weren't allowed to put it there. Even after Baltimore Gas and Electric went to court and got a ruling saying that they could place the pole where they wanted to, she staged a peaceful protest: When the workers showed up to put in the pole, they found Annie sitting in her rocking chair on the designated spot. She refused to move. She sat in that chair every day for three days, until the workmen gave up and moved the light to a different location down the block.

This was the family that Thurgood Marshall was born into: a group of intelligent, opinionated, stubborn people who valued education and fought for their beliefs. One more strong influence on Thurgood was his father's interest in the law. Willie, in his spare time, liked to go to the local courthouse and sit in on trials. He was fascinated by the justice system and liked to study how different lawyers presented and argued their cases. Often, he would take his sons with him. He liked to talk about politics, social issues, and the law at home, and he encouraged his sons to participate—as long as they could back up their opinions with facts and strong arguments. Thurgood Marshall once said, "[My father] never told me to become a lawyer, but he turned me into one. He did it by teaching me to argue, by challenging my logic on every point, by making me prove every statement I made."

Another important step in Marshall's path toward the Supreme Court happened fairly early in his life. In elementary school, he displayed what could politely be called a spirited and mischievous persona. Put simply, he got into trouble a lot. The principal of the school had a unique method of punishment for habitual troublemakers. He would force them to sit in a room in the basement with a copy of the United States Constitution and make them memorize a passage. Because Marshall was punished so often, he memorized quite a bit of it. In fact, to give an idea of the number of times he must have gotten in trouble in school, he once told a reporter, "Before I left school, I knew the entire Constitution by heart."

He may have been lighthearted about it in his later years, but it was that knowledge of the Constitution, and especially the Fourteenth Amendment, that opened his eyes to the importance of justice in the world. The Fourteenth Amendment was created just after the end of the Civil War, when Americans had a lot of questions regarding the former Confederates and the status of ex-slaves in the country. Its main purpose was to ensure that the Civil Rights Act passed in 1866 was upheld. The Thirteenth Amendment had officially ended slavery; now the Fourteenth was designed to detail the rights of these newly freed people. In addition to forbidding any state to deny citizens their rights regarding life issues, property, and due process, it also gave citizens the right to equality. The equal protection clause says that states cannot deny any person within their **jurisdiction** the equal protection of the laws. In other words, all citizens of the United States, regardless of their race, are guaranteed the same civil rights and civil liberties. They are all to be treated equally and given the same privileges.

Yet, Marshall grew up in the years closely following the Supreme Court's *Plessy v. Ferguson* decision, which was handed down after a mixed-race man named Homer Plessy challenged a Louisiana law that **stipulated** separate trains cars for white and colored people. The law said that the cars must be equal in facilities, and banned whites from sitting in black cars in addition to prohibiting blacks from sitting in white cars. Plessy, who was seven-eighths white and one-eighth black, sat in a vacant seat in a whites-only car and was arrested and imprisoned. After he was convicted, Plessy filed a petition against the judge in that trial at the Louisiana Supreme Court, saying that the train car law violated the equal protection clause of the Fourteenth Amendment.

The Supreme Court actually ruled against him, saying that the equality promised by the Fourteenth Amendment extended only to political and civil rights, and not to "social rights," such as where to sit on a train. They rejected Plessy's argument that the law marked blacks "with a badge of inferiority," pointing out that both blacks and whites were provided with equal facilities under the law. Because of this ruling, until the middle of the twentieth century, *Plessy v. Ferguson* laid the groundwork for "separate but equal" facilities, allowing racial segregation in public places and shutting down legal challenges against segregated institutions throughout the South. The problem, of course, was that the facilities and institutions allotted to African Americans were decidedly inferior to those used by white people.

Thurgood Marshall couldn't help but notice the problems with the supposed "separate but equal" facilities around him. Although he had friends of both races, he lived in a black neighborhood and attended a black school. The white school, for the white families who lived in white neighborhoods, was visibly nicer and better equipped.

Still, he enjoyed popularity in high school, where he had both male and female friends, served on the student council, and became captain of the debating team. The personality traits he exhibited here would surface in his adult years: the ability to get along well and relate to people, the willingness to work with others, and the skills to present a logical argument based on fact.

In high school, Marshall wasn't a straight-A student. He still had the tendency to misbehave, and he didn't take his studies entirely seriously. However, he knew he was expected to go to college, and when the time came, he chose Lincoln University in Chester, Pennsylvania. Founded in 1857, it was one of the oldest colleges for African Americans in the United States. Not only did it have a reputation for turning out professionals, like doctors, lawyers, and scientists, but Aubrey, his older brother, was already a student there.

Marshall had been working summers at the B&O Railroad to try to save money for college, but when the time came, he was short of the funds he needed to pay his tuition. Norma took matters into her own hands. She **pawned** her engagement and wedding rings to get enough money to make up the difference. Off to Lincoln he went.

A New Chapter

Was it in college that young Thurgood Marshall began to show signs of the great man he would become? Not exactly. He seemed to enjoy playing cards more than going to class, and while he also starred on the debate team, he was actually suspended from the school twice for pulling pranks on other students. One of his classmates, writer Langston Hughes, once referred to him as being "rough and ready, loud and wrong." Yet Marshall started to realize that he wanted to make changes in the world. Hughes was one of the people who helped him to think differently about what he could do with his life.

Many of the professors at Lincoln were Ivy League graduates, coming from Harvard, Princeton, and Yale. They were also all white. In one of his classes, the students discussed whether the school should hire black teachers. Marshall was one of the majority of students who voted against this suggestion. Why would African-American students be against being taught by African-American professors? Some of them simply didn't want change. Others said that the students wouldn't respect black teachers. Langston Hughes was angry when he found out how Marshall had voted. He confronted Marshall and asked him why he would be upset over being discriminated against in a movie theater while he himself discriminated against black professors. Marshall saw the wisdom in this, and the two discussed racial issues many times afterward.

The incident to which Hughes referred took place one afternoon when Marshall and a group of his classmates went to see a movie at a local theater. After they bought their tickets and went to sit down in the main area of the movie house, an usher told them they had to go sit up in the balcony. The floor seats, which were better, were reserved for white people. Marshall and his friends asked for their ticket money back, but the usher refused. Insulted and angry, the students pulled down the theater's curtains and broke the front door on their way out.

This wasn't the only time Marshall had faced blatant racism in his life, of course. When he was only fourteen, he'd been arrested for punching a white man who called him a "nigger." In Marshall's defense, his father had told him that punching the other person was the appropriate response to being called such a horrible name. During the months that he worked on the B&O Railroad, he was not allowed to join a **union**, which would have helped him get better pay and benefits, because he was black. He was also denied overtime pay for the same reason.

A New Love, A New Direction

One of the most positive changes in Marshall's life happened in college: he met his future wife, Vivian "Buster" Burey. Whether it was her direct influence or his desire to impress her, the result was the same: he buckled down and started to take his studies seriously. He also became a star member of the debate team, where, he said later, he learned to spot the weaknesses in his opponents' arguments and figure out how to use them to his advantage.

Thurgood Marshall and Vivian Burey were married in 1929, before either of them had graduated from college. The following year, when he returned to campus, he also returned to the issue of whether Lincoln should hire black professors. He convinced his reluctant classmates by arguing that a college degree was meaningless if it didn't even qualify them to teach at their own **alma mater**. When a

Jazz musician Cab Calloway
(*left*) and poet Langston Hughes
(*right*) were two of Marshall's
most famous college classmates.

FAMOUS FRIENDS

Thurgood Marshall attended college at Lincoln University with several other prominent African Americans, including the future president of Kenya, but two of his classmates were professionals of a different type. Langston Hughes became a well-known writer as one of the leading voices in the Harlem Renaissance. He wrote books for both adults and children—poems, nonfiction, and more—mostly on topics regarding the treatment of minorities and the fight for equality. Cab Calloway, who had plans to attend law school, went on instead to become a celebrated jazz entertainer. He was one of the world's most famous bandleaders for many years. He and his musicians took over as house band at the world-famous Cotton Club in Harlem after Duke Ellington and his orchestra vacated the position.

vote was next taken on the issue, the majority of students voted to integrate the faculty. Marshall was learning how to influence others with both facts and feelings.

Marshall graduated in 1930, and he and Buster moved back to Baltimore to live with Marshall's parents while they tried to figure out what they wanted to do next. When Marshall decided that he wanted to go to law school, he knew which school was his first choice: the University of Maryland.

By the time he graduated from Lincoln, Marshall was an honor student. In addition to the debate team, he excelled in other extracurricular activities. He was the kind of young man that any law school would have been happy to have—but the University of Maryland wouldn't accept his application because he was African American. Angry and disappointed, Marshall applied to Howard University's law school. It didn't have a reputation for having the best students, but it turned out to be the right place for Marshall at the right time.

First, the new dean of the school, Charles Hamilton Houston, eased some of Marshall's fears by announcing that he intended to implement stricter academic standards at the school. He wanted to improve its reputation, and he told the students that two-thirds of them might fail their first year if they couldn't keep up with the scholastic expectations. Marshall rose to the occasion and worked to become the top student in his class. He was too poor to afford rent in Washington, DC, so he took the train to and from Baltimore every day and used the time to study.

Second, Houston became an important mentor and advisor to Marshall. He was a graduate of Amherst College who had earned his law degree at Harvard. In becoming the dean of Howard Law School, he hoped to educate and train highly skilled lawyers to fight Jim Crow laws in courts all across the country. To show them what kinds of battles they'd be fighting, he took the students to jails and police stations as well as courthouses. He also asked good students like Thurgood Marshall to help out on real cases. His goal was to

Charles Hamilton Houston and his father, preparing for a civil rights case.

Thurgood Marshall: The First African-American Supreme Court Justice

teach them to become what he called "social engineers," people who would fight to make changes in society and give African Americans the chance for a better life. Marshall took this lesson to heart.

Third, Marshall earned a job at the law library, and while working there, he met many people who worked for the NAACP, who used the library with Houston's encouragement to research cases. They got to know Marshall and noticed his intelligence and talents, so he was sometimes recruited to help them with their research.

Once Marshall graduated in 1933 at the top of his class, he returned to Baltimore and opened his own one-man law firm. His office was furnished with castoffs from his parents' home, and sometimes clients were hard to come by. In his spare time, he worked for the local chapter of the NAACP. A woman named Lillie Jackson was now director of the Baltimore NAACP, and she asked Marshall to help her repair its reputation. Black people were often afraid to hire black lawyers because of the prejudices of the courts, but Thurgood Marshall knew how to talk to people and relate to them. He would establish a **rapport** so that despite his education and his fledgling career, they felt that he could relate to them and their struggles.

Marshall and the NAACP

In the meantime, Charles Hamilton Houston had also begun working for the NAACP, which was already strategizing ways to strike down *Plessy v. Ferguson* and segregation and inequality in American schools. He would take Marshall with him on fact-finding missions to the Deep South, where they saw for themselves what poor shape most black schools were in and how disadvantaged the children and families were.

In 1934, Marshall scored one of his first major successes in the courtroom. The NAACP asked him to represent a black man accused of killing a white man. This was one of the most serious crimes a black man could commit in the eyes of the white community. Marshall convinced the jury that the police had beaten his client's confession out of him, and they found the man not guilty of murder. Instead, they convicted him of manslaughter. This was a tremendous triumph, and not only for the man accused, who received a much lighter sentence. Marshall had proved that a black lawyer could get a white jury to listen.

He soon took on another case that made history: Marshall became the first black lawyer to defend a white client. The white man, a Maryland attorney named Bernard Ades, got in trouble with a local judge for accusing the judge of not giving his black client a fair trial. Judge William Coleman took action to have Ades **disbarred**. Luckily, by the time the case became active, Judge Coleman had **recused** himself from the case and Marshall was able to convince the new judge to allow Ades to keep his law license.

However, success in the courtroom had not led to financial success for Marshall. He was struggling to pay his bills when Houston made him an offer in 1936: Would he like to move to New York City and take over the NAACP's office there? Eager to take advantage of having a steady income as well as the chance to do more for the organization, Marshall and Vivian packed their bags and moved to Harlem. Once there, they would enjoy the fruits of the Harlem Renaissance—the art, literature, music, and nightlife it provided.

For the next eighteen years, Marshall won many significant cases and moved up in the ranks of the NAACP. By 1940, just four years after taking the job in New York City, he became the chief of the NAACP Legal Defense and Educational Fund.

In 1946, he won the Spingarn Medal, which the NAACP awards annually for outstanding achievement by an African American. But his greatest courtroom victory came in 1954, when Marshall overturned *Plessy v. Ferguson* in the Supreme Court and thus ensured his place in the history books. His arguments in the case, *Brown v. Board of Education of Topeka, Kansas*, and the language of the decision are still studied by law students today.

Four years after the initial decision, Marshall returned to the Supreme Court in 1958 to continue to fight for the promises made in *Brown v. Board of Education*.

A Personal Tragedy, and a New Beginning

However, this professional triumph was soon followed by a personal tragedy. Vivian, his wife of twenty-five years, told him that she had terminal cancer. She hadn't wanted to tell him sooner, so as not to distract him from his important work on the *Brown* case. Marshall immediately took a six-week sabbatical from work to help take care of Vivian in her final days. She died at the age of forty-four, and those who knew Marshall said he was devastated by the loss. He took the first vacation of his life in the aftermath of her death and traveled to Mexico.

Eleven months later, in December 1955, he got remarried to a woman named Cecilia "Cissy" Suyat. Cissy worked as a secretary at the NAACP's New York headquarters, so they had known each other for some time. His friends were happy for him, despite the short length of time between Vivian's death and his marriage to Cissy. They said he was the type of person who needed to be married.

One of the greatest blessings of his second marriage was the two sons he had with Cissy: Thurgood Junior, who was born in 1956, and John, who was born in 1958. Marshall enjoyed spending more time at home to be with them, and he shared his longstanding love of trains with them. In later years, when the family lived in Alexandria, Virginia, the Marshalls would host backyard barbecues for the neighborhood, with the judge himself manning the grill.

In 1961, President John F. Kennedy appointed Marshall to the Second Circuit Court of Appeals in New York. This was an honor for Marshall and a giant step forward for the African-American community, few of whom had achieved the status of judge. In 1965, though, Marshall achieved something even bigger: President Lyndon B. Johnson asked Marshall to serve as the first African-American US solicitor general, the attorney who argues before the Supreme Court on behalf of the federal government. Little did Marshall know that Johnson had even bigger plans for him in the near future.

Thurgood and Cecilia Marshall with their two sons, circa 1961.

In the meantime, over the next two years, Marshall won fourteen of the nineteen cases that he argued before the Supreme Court.

President Lyndon B. Johnson was an advocate for civil rights himself. He was instrumental in championing and passing the 1964 Civil Rights Act and the 1965 Voting Rights Act. He told J. Edgar Hoover, the head of the Federal Bureau of Investigation (FBI), to stop going after communists and civil rights activists and focus on stopping the Ku Klux Klan. He also made it a point to hire black people for high-ranking positions in his administration. He appointed an African-American man, Robert C. Weaver, to be the United States' secretary of housing and urban development (HUD), making him the first black person to serve as an officer in a president's cabinet. In another first for African Americans, he asked US Army major Hugh Robinson to serve as one of his military aides. Johnson's plan with the most far-reaching effects, though, was his intention to name the first African-American justice to the Supreme Court.

In 1967, Justice Tom C. Clark decided to retire from the bench, and at a ceremony in the Rose Garden on the White House grounds, Johnson nominated Marshall with these words:

> I have just talked to the Chief Justice and informed him that I shall send to the Senate this afternoon the nomination of Mr. Thurgood Marshall, Solicitor General, to the position of Associate Justice of the Supreme Court made vacant by the resignation of Justice Tom C. Clark of Texas …
>
> I believe he earned that appointment; he deserves the appointment. He is best qualified by training and by very valuable service to the country. I believe it is the right thing to do, the right time to do it, the right man and the right place.

After a **grueling** confirmation session under the US Senate, Thurgood Marshall was confirmed as the United States Supreme

Mourners file past Marshall's casket, which lay in state in the Great Hall of the Supreme Court after Marshall's death in 1993.

Court's ninety-sixth justice and its first African-American justice. He served in this role for twenty-four years, only retiring because his health was failing.

When Thurgood Marshall died in 1993, at the age of eighty-four, his casket lay in state in the Great Hall of the Supreme Court. More than twenty thousand mourners, including political leaders, judges, and journalists, paid their respects. He is buried in Arlington National Cemetery, the final resting place of presidents, politicians, and eleven other Supreme Court justices, as well as the hundreds of thousands of military personnel who also served the United States.

CHAPTER THREE

⌣

His Contemporaries

When it comes to contemporaries in the law, Thurgood Marshall had few. He was a man of many firsts, a trailblazer for African Americans, and a high achiever. However, he was influenced by a small group of lawyers and activists with whom he worked in order to overturn the discriminatory Jim Crow laws.

Charles Hamilton Houston

One man who certainly led the way for Marshall was his mentor and later coworker, Charles Hamilton Houston. Once nicknamed "The Man Who Killed Jim Crow," Houston played a part in nearly every civil rights case brought before the Supreme Court between 1930 and 1954, when his protégé, Thurgood

A formal portrait of Charles Hamilton Houston, Marshall's mentor.

Marshall, won the landmark case *Brown v. Board of Education*. Houston planned to abolish Jim Crow segregation by eroding the power of *Plessy v. Ferguson* one case at a time.

Only thirteen years Marshall's senior, Houston was a native of Washington, DC, who was inspired to study the law after serving in the segregated army during World War I. During his time in the army, he saw how his fellow African-American service members were discriminated against and, especially, how they could be convicted of crimes not due to any evidence against them, but because of their race. He once wrote:

> The hate and scorn showered on us Negro officers by our fellow Americans convinced me that there was no sense in my dying for a world ruled by them. I made up my mind that if I got through this war I would study law and use my time fighting for men who could not strike back.

Before joining the army, he had graduated Phi Beta Kappa from Amherst College, then taught English at Howard University. When he completed his service with the army, he attended Harvard Law School, where he became the first African-American editor of the *Harvard Law Review*. Not content with a regular law degree, he went on to earn a Doctor of Juridical Science (SJD), Harvard Law School's most advanced law degree, which was another first for an African American. In the early days of his practice, he went back to Washington, DC, and joined his father's law firm, which became Houston and Houston.

In Washington, Houston also joined the faculty of Howard University's law school. While there, he taught students, including Thurgood Marshall, to use the law to fight against racial discrimination. Houston was instrumental not only in educating Marshall but also in promoting his career with the NAACP, which eventually led to Marshall's appointment to the Supreme Court.

In 1935, Houston left Howard and joined the NAACP as their attorney. His goal was to head its legal attack on Jim Crow laws. His strategy was to build a foundation of legal precedents against "separate but equal" education for African Americans. In 1938, he successfully argued before the Supreme Court that it was unconstitutional for a state to give an African-American student funds for an out-of-state law school instead of allowing the student to attend the only law school in the state.

After Houston turned over the NAACP's legal leadership to Thurgood Marshall, he continued to work toward improved rights for African Americans. He won two cases before the Supreme Court in 1944: *Steele v. Louisville & Nashville Railroad Co.* and *Tunstall v. Brotherhood of Locomotive Firemen and Enginemen.* In these cases, the court ruled that railway unions needed to fairly represent African-American employees. Houston again triumphed before the court in 1948, in the case of *Hurd v. Hodge*, when the justices ruled that racial discrimination could not influence the sale of property.

Sadly, Houston died in 1950, long before seeing his fight against "separate but equal" facilities won by his former student Thurgood Marshall. Marshall was quick to credit him at the hour of his victory, saying that Houston was the one who had set him on the right course to win the landmark case: "We wouldn't have been any place if Charlie hadn't laid the groundwork for it."

Houston **posthumously** won the NAACP's Spingarn Medal, which recognizes top achievers in the African-American community. Two buildings are named in his honor: the Charles Hamilton Houston Institute for Race and Justice at Harvard Law School and Charles Hamilton Houston Hall, the main building at Howard University's law school. In addition, there is a professorship at Harvard Law named after him—and one of its recipients, Elena Kagan, served as the dean of Harvard Law School before becoming the Supreme Court's fourth female justice in 2010.

Wade Hampton McCree

If Charles Hamilton Houston helped to inspire Thurgood Marshall, Marshall, in turn, inspired countless others. One of those who benefitted from Marshall's trailblazing was Wade Hampton McCree Jr. Born just twelve years after Marshall, McCree also became an attorney, a judge, and a public official. Just as Marshall served as the first African American on the US Court of Appeals for the Second Circuit, McCree was the first African American appointed to the Sixth Circuit, which has jurisdiction over district courts in Kentucky, Michigan, Ohio, and Tennessee.

Like Marshall, McCree caught the attention of Presidents Kennedy and Johnson in the 1960s. President Kennedy nominated him to the United States District Court for the Eastern District of Michigan in 1961, which was a first for an African American. President Johnson was the one who nominated McCree to the United States Court of Appeals in 1966. Like Houston, McCree served in the United States Army and graduated from Harvard Law School.

McCree became the second African-American solicitor general in the history of the United States, from 1977 to 1981, after which he left government service and became a law school professor. He taught at the University of Michigan Law School until he died in 1987.

Oliver Hill

One man whose work has unfortunately been overshadowed by Thurgood Marshall's is Oliver Hill, the second-ranked student in the Howard University School of Law class of 1933. Charles Hamilton Houston also enlisted Hill to work on his legal cases for the NAACP, and Hill's achievements were quite impressive on their own.

Born in Richmond, Virginia, in 1907, Hill earned his undergraduate degree from Howard University before entering the law school. Like Thurgood Marshall, he was inspired by Houston

Wade Hampton McCree, the first African-American federal judge in the Eastern District of Michigan and the second African-American United States solicitor general.

and Houston's concept of social engineering. He worked together with Marshall on many cases for the NAACP (and later, the Legal Defense Fund), including the *Brown* case. In fact, he served as head attorney for one of the cases that would be incorporated into the larger *Brown* case, *Davis v. County School Board of Prince Edward County*.

Hill also worked with Marshall and others on *Alston v. School Board of Norfolk, Virginia*, a 1940 court case against unequal pay for black and white teachers. A few years later, he won the right for equal transportation for school children from the Virginia Supreme Court. He continued to chip away at school segregation in Virginia throughout the 1940s, and in 1949, he became the first African American on the City Council of Richmond, Virginia.

He may not be as well known as his classmate, but Hill received numerous professional awards and honors. In 1959, the National Bar Association anointed him "Lawyer of the Year." In 1986, the NAACP Legal Defense and Educational Fund gave him the Simple Justice Award. Seven years later, he won the American Bar Association Justice Thurgood Marshall Award, which "recognizes long-term contributions by members of the legal profession to the advancement of civil rights, civil liberties, and human rights in the United States." In July 2000, Hill received the American Bar

THE NATIONAL ASSOCIATION FOR THE ADVANCEMENT OF COLORED PEOPLE

The NAACP has been in existence since 1909, founded partially in response to the ongoing violence perpetrated against African Americans, such as lynchings, and the 1908 race riot in Springfield, Illinois. Its founding members were both black and white and included famous names such as Mary White Ovington and W. E. B. Du Bois. The NAACP's continuing mission is to "ensure the political, educational, social, and economic equality of rights of all persons and to eliminate race-based discrimination." Its members "envision a society in which all individuals have equal rights without discrimination based on race."

When Thurgood Marshall became the head of the NAACP's legal arm in 1940, he spun it off into the NAACP Legal Defense and Educational Fund (LDF). As head of the LDF, he brought thirty-two cases before the Supreme Court, including *Brown v. Board of Education*. Now known as the country's first and foremost civil and human rights law firm, the LDF's mission is to seek structural change, expand democracy, eliminate disparities, and achieve racial justice through litigation, advocacy, and public education. The LDF also "defends the gains and protections won over the past seventy-five years of civil rights struggle and works to improve the quality and diversity of judicial and executive appointments."

Oliver Hill, the first African American to be elected to the Richmond, Virginia, city council.

Association Medal, the highest honor bestowed by the ABA, because he had "toiled for more than two generations to make equality and justice living realities for all the people of the United States."

Hill has been honored in his home state by having a building named after him. The Oliver W. Hill Building is the first building in Virginia's Capitol Square to be named for an African American. Finally, on August 11, 1999, President William J. Clinton presented Hill with the highest honor the United States can bestow upon a civilian, the Presidential Medal of Freedom.

Not content to rest on his laurels, however, Oliver Hill remained active in civil rights activities until his death in 2007.

The Supreme Court Justices

When Thurgood Marshall joined the Supreme Court, the eight other men already serving were Chief Justice Earl Warren, Hugo Black,

THE CONSTITUTION
OF THE UNITED STATES
OF AMERICA

The Constitution is the source of all laws in the United States. Through it, government powers are specified, providing authority as well as limitations to protect the fundamental rights of United States citizens. Most people are familiar with the preamble, which begins with the phrase "We the people of the United States" and continues:

> in Order to form a more perfect Union, establish Justice, insure domestic Tranquility, provide for the common defense, promote the general Welfare, and secure the Blessings of Liberty to ourselves and our Posterity, do ordain and establish this Constitution for the United States of America.

The first ten amendments, or changes, to the Constitution later became known as the Bill of Rights. The Thirteenth, Fourteenth, and Fifteenth Amendments became known as the Reconstruction Amendments because they were passed after the Civil War to ensure political equality for all Americans, including the newly freed slaves. The Thirteenth Amendment abolishes slavery or involuntary servitude except in punishment for a crime. The Fourteenth Amendment defines all people born in the United States as citizens, requires due process of law, and requires equal protection for all people. The Fifteenth Amendment prevents the denial of a citizen's vote based on race, color, or previous condition of servitude.

William O. Douglas, John Marshall Harlan, William Brennan, Potter Stewart, Byron White, and Abe Fortas. Warren, Black, and Douglas had been on the court in 1954, when they voted in Marshall's favor in *Brown v. Board of Education*, so they were familiar with him and his work.

As chief justice, Earl Warren was the one who swore Marshall in. He also was tasked with reading out the court's decision in *Brown v. Board of Education*. Justice Warren presided over the Supreme Court during a period of tremendous changes in the United States, when the court had to rule on the constitutionality of cases in the areas of race relations, criminal procedure, and legislative apportionment. Like Marshall, Warren leaned toward the liberal side. He thought it was appropriate for the court to assist in and enforce social change, especially in the areas of civil liberties and civil rights. Warren liked to find potential solutions to contemporary social problems within the Constitution.

Before being appointed to the Supreme Court, Warren served in the army during World War I, went to law school, served as a district attorney in Alameda County, California, and later became governor of the state for three terms. Even then, he was considered socially progressive.

In 1953, President Dwight D. Eisenhower nominated Warren to be the chief justice of the US Supreme Court. It was only a year later that he heard the *Brown* case. When the court made its unanimous decision, it was Warren who spoke for them, declaring that the separation of public-school children according to race was unconstitutional. In their rejection of the "separate but equal" doctrine established by *Plessy v. Ferguson* in 1896, the court stated that "separate educational facilities are inherently unequal," and called for the desegregation of public schools with "all deliberate speed." In his opinion on the case, Warren wrote:

> Segregation of white and colored children in public schools has a detrimental effect upon the colored

The justices of the 1953 Supreme Court, who heard the arguments in *Brown v. Board of Education*. Chief Justice Earl Warren is seated in the center of the first row.

children. The impact is greater when it has the sanction of the law, for the policy of separating the races is usually interpreted as denoting the inferiority of the Negro group ... Any language in contrary to this finding is rejected. We conclude that in the field of public education the doctrine of "separate but equal" has no place. Separate educational facilities are inherently unequal.

Warren retired from the Supreme Court in 1969 after serving for sixteen years. Because the two so often voted the same, Marshall became discouraged after Warren's departure when the makeup of the court became more conservative. When Warren died in 1974, Marshall was quoted in the *New York Times* as saying, "When history is written, he'll go down as one of the greatest chief justices the country has ever been blessed with."

Hugo Black had one of the more unlikely backgrounds for a Supreme Court justice. Born in the Deep South, in Harlan, Alabama, he graduated Phi Beta Kappa from the University of Alabama School of Law in 1906. In the early 1920s, he joined the Ku Klux Klan (KKK). At this point in history, the Klan was not only anti-black but rallied against foreigners, Jews, and Roman Catholics. They held marches and rallies and even parades across the country, and adopted the burning cross as a symbol.

However, Black openly opposed the Klan's activities and claimed that he only joined because he needed their support if he wanted to be a successful politician in the South. He quit the KKK after two years, just before running for office as a US senator. When President Franklin D. Roosevelt nominated Black, who had always been one of his biggest supporters, for the Supreme Court in 1937, people remembered Black's years of KKK membership and were outraged.

As a Supreme Court justice, Black tended to vote in favor of civil rights. Despite his literal interpretation of the US Constitution, he was considered a liberal in his decisions.

John Marshall Harlan II was the grandson and namesake of John Marshall Harlan I, who also served as a Supreme Court Justice from 1877 to 1911. The elder Harlan was known for **dissenting** on many of the court's cases in his early days—usually siding against his colleagues in support of civil rights. He was the only justice to oppose the 1883 decision to strike down the Civil Rights Act of 1875, and the only one to oppose the ruling in *Plessy v. Ferguson*.

Fifty-eight years later, the appointment of his grandson to the court was delayed because his nomination encountered resistance from Southerners. They feared that the younger Harlan might share his grandfather's well-known hostility to legalized segregation, and they hoped that delaying his confirmation might keep the court from implementing *Brown v. Board of Education*. The second Justice Harlan did not focus on civil rights, although he was personally committed to racial justice. He was legally conservative, and he was as much of a dissenter as his grandfather, but his disagreements with the more liberal members of the Warren Court tended to stem from his belief that they were wrong to expand the role and power of the federal judiciary and reduce the autonomy of the states.

William Brennan was another known liberal justice on the court. He served for more than thirty-three years. A graduate of Harvard Law School and a veteran of World War II, he won positions on both the Superior Court and the Supreme Court of his home state of New Jersey. As a US Supreme Court justice, Brennan made it clear that he believed in the fundamental rights of individuals. He supported court rulings in favor of affirmative action, gender equality, and abortion rights. Although he was a Roman Catholic, Brennan believed in the division of church and state. He also vehemently opposed the death penalty, citing its constitutional violations. Following *Brown v. Board of Education*, Justice Brennan wrote several opinions that were crucial in ensuring that the principles of the *Brown* decision were carried out.

In an address to the Bar Association of the City of New York, Brennan once said that constitutional interpretation "demands of judges more than proficiency in logical analysis. It requires that we be sensitive to the balance of reason and passion that mark a given age, and the ways in which that balance leaves its mark on the everyday exchanges between government and citizen."

When President Clinton awarded him the Presidential Medal of Freedom in 1993, he remarked:

> [Justice Brennan] once said the role of the Constitution is the protection of the dignity of every human being and he recognized that every individual has fundamental human

rights that government cannot deny. He spent a lifetime upholding those rights and he offered some of the most enduring constitutional decisions of this century.

William O. Douglas, nominated by President Roosevelt in 1939 when he was forty, was the second-youngest Supreme Court justice in US history. He also served the longest of any justice. Douglas sat on the bench for thirty-six years, serving under five different chief justices. He retired in 1975. During his tenure, he advocated for civil liberties and often allied himself with Hugo Black, both of them championing the Bill of Rights. He believed in free speech, freedom of the press, and the constitutional rights of criminal suspects.

Justices White, Stewart, and Fortas were not well known for their opinions on civil rights cases. They all had other areas where they preferred to lead. Justice Stewart, for example, was best known for his contributions to criminal justice reform. Justice White was extremely conservative and famously dissented on some of the court's most famous decisions, including *Miranda v. Arizona* and *Roe v. Wade*. Abraham Fortas only served on the court for four years. He resigned after he was threatened with impeachment.

Whether as an attorney arguing before the justices of the Supreme Court or as a justice himself, Thurgood Marshall more than earned his nickname of "Mr. Civil Rights." He owed that nickname in part, though, to the men he studied under and worked with. From his mentor, Charles Hamilton Houston, to his colleagues in law and the Supreme Court, he found support in his relentless efforts to ensure that the powers of the Constitution were used to protect African Americans and other minorities.

CHAPTER FOUR

A Professional Life in Pursuit of a Singular Goal

Before examining Thurgood Marshall's most famous case, it's important to go back and look at some of the other significant cases he worked on in the years leading up to *Brown v. Board of Education of Topeka, Kansas*. Between the strong influence of his mentor, Charles Hamilton Houston, and his family, who taught Marshall to stand up for what was right, a definite pattern emerged early on in his career. These cases paved the way for the *Brown* case—and the end of Jim Crow.

Linda Brown (*center*), seated in her segregated classroom.

Young Thurgood Marshall with his client Donald Gaines Murray, who, like Marshall, was rejected by the University of Maryland Law School simply for being African American.

1936 and 1938:
Murray v. Maryland and *Gaines v. Missouri*

The case *Murray v. Maryland* is significant for a number of reasons. First, Thurgood Marshall was particularly invested in this case because he was still angry that the law school of the University of Maryland had rejected him based on the color of his skin. When he found another potential law student who had been turned down by UMD's law school, he volunteered to sue the school on the student's behalf.

Donald Murray, like Marshall, had been an honor student in college. As a Maryland native, he wanted to stay close to home and go to law school at the state university. He wrote to the school, asking for admissions information, and the president of the school responded by saying that they did not enroll African-American students. He suggested that Murray apply to an out-of-state law school set up for African Americans, called the Princess Anne Academy and sponsored by the University of Maryland. He even said that Murray could get a scholarship to go there.

But Murray didn't want to go to Princess Anne Academy. He wanted to go to UMD. When Marshall sued the university for him, he said that Princess Anne Academy was not equal to UMD's law school. It had fewer teachers, smaller facilities, and far less funding. It was not even close in quality to UMD. He also proved that the school rejected Murray simply on the basis of his race. The president admitted it, and the letter the school had sent Murray said, "The University of Maryland does not admit Negro students and your application is accordingly rejected." Marshall argued that the policy contradicted the Fourteenth Amendment and was therefore discriminatory. The judge agreed and ordered UMD to admit Murray to its law school.

This was an enormous legal victory for African Americans nationwide—and a source of personal satisfaction for Thurgood Marshall. On the other hand, because he had won the case, Marshall couldn't go through the **appeals** system in the hopes that it would wind up in front of the Supreme Court. That was the ultimate goal: to try a similar case and have it taken up by the Supreme Court, in the hopes that such an event would change the law for the entire country.

Soon enough, he and Houston found another African-American man who wanted to go to his state's law school. Lloyd Gaines wanted to attend the University of Missouri, but like Donald Murray, he was rejected because of his race. However, Gaines had a few more obstacles that Marshall had to overcome. First, some of the out-of-state law schools to which Missouri sent its black students were actually nearly equivalent to the University of Missouri. Second, the university claimed that they were willing to build a separate, in-state law school for African-American students. That was alright, though, because Marshall and Houston wanted to lose. That way, they could plead Gaines's case in front of the Supreme Court and hopefully score a victory that would have a national impact.

Their strategy was to argue for *Plessy v. Ferguson*. By reminding the court to uphold that ruling, they'd establish the right to sue a state if it didn't make its school for blacks equal to those for whites. It worked. The Gaines decision meant that each state had to either build a separate graduate school for blacks or integrate. Marshall knew that most states would not be able to afford to build all new schools, so they'd be forced to admit African-American students into their white schools. His victory here was a major stepping stone on the journey to *Brown v. Board of Education of Topeka, Kansas.*

1941: *Smith v. Allwright*

Marshall once called *Smith v. Allwright* the most important case of his career, although it is not nearly as well known as some others he won. He had been working to secure voting rights for African Americans in the South. Remember, the Fifteenth Amendment to the Constitution, ratified in 1870, explicitly granted African Americans the right to vote. The people in power in the South, however, tried to avoid giving them that right by levying poll taxes or threatening physical violence. Another tactic was keeping African Americans from voting in primary elections, which they called "the white primary."

Earlier in the year, Marshall and another lawyer named W. J. Durham had filed a lawsuit against the Texas Democratic Party because they refused to let black people vote in primary elections. That case got thrown out on a technicality, so Marshall had to find someone else who would challenge the status quo. A doctor named Lonnie Smith agreed to contest the voting limitation. A white election official named S. S. Allwright denied Smith the right to vote in the 1940 Texas Democratic primary, and Marshall took the case. Although he lost at the state level, he knew this would give him a chance to appeal to a higher court.

It took until 1943 for the case to be argued in front of the Supreme Court, but Marshall was victorious. The Supreme Court agreed that prohibiting African Americans from voting in primary elections was a violation of the Constitution. In their official ruling, they wrote:

> The right to vote in a primary for the nomination of candidates without discrimination by the State, like the right to vote in a general election, is a right secured by the Constitution.

Smith v. Allwright was a major victory for civil rights because it established that every American adult, regardless of color, had the right to participate in all aspects of the election process. It also gave African Americans the incentive to care about the US political system, now that they had a voice in it. The NAACP also enjoyed positive publicity from the case, as the media realized how hard they had worked to establish and protect the rights of minorities. Marshall himself became somewhat of a celebrity after winning. Most importantly, he knew that the ruling could have an influence on future cases at all levels of the legal system and in the writing or revising of laws.

1946: *Morgan v. Virginia*

Jim Crow laws were still going strong in the spring of 1946, when a black woman named Irene Morgan got onto a bus in Virginia to travel to Baltimore, Maryland. When she was ordered to sit in the back of the bus, as Virginia state law dictated, she questioned this order. She said that since the bus was going on an interstate journey, the Virginia law did not apply. Morgan was arrested.

Marshall took on her case, with the backing of the NAACP. His argument was that since an 1877 Supreme Court decision ruled that it was illegal for a state to forbid segregation, it was also illegal for a state to require it. He won. In its ruling, the Supreme Court stated:

> As no state law can reach beyond its own border nor bar transportation of passengers across its boundaries, diverse seating requirements for the races in interstate journeys result. As there is no federal act dealing with the separation of races in interstate transportation, we must decide the validity of this Virginia statute on the challenge that it interferes with commerce, as a matter of balance between the exercise of the local police power and the need for national uniformity in the

regulations for interstate travel. It seems clear to us that seating arrangements for the different races in interstate motor travel require a single, uniform rule to promote and protect national travel. Consequently, we hold the Virginia statute in controversy invalid.

However, because the court did not rule that segregated transportation within the state was unconstitutional, bus companies still segregated passengers until the civil rights laws passed in the 1960s put an end to it once and for all.

1947: *Patton v. Mississippi*

While Marshall tended to focus on cases concerning education or voting rights, he did occasionally take on criminal cases. In 1947, a black man named Eddie Patton was put on trial for killing a white man, and was convicted—but by an all-white jury. Marshall, with the backing of the NAACP, challenged that conviction, saying that Patton could not have gotten a fair trial under those circumstances. He first argued it in front of the Mississippi State Trial Court, then the Mississippi State Supreme Court. Finally, when he brought the case before the Supreme Court, they agreed that juries could not convict African-American defendants if African Americans had been denied the chance to serve on the juries.

1948: *Shelley v. Kraemer*

In his childhood, Thurgood Marshall had noticed that black families and white families tended to live in separate neighborhoods. What he probably didn't know back then was that some white communities instituted laws that prohibited black families from moving in. The case of *Shelley v. Kraemer* gave Marshall the opportunity to fight that sort of enforced segregation.

The Shelleys were an African-American family who purchased a home in a residential neighborhood in Missouri. Unfortunately, this neighborhood had set up a racially restrictive **covenant**. This meant that all neighborhood residents agreed not to sell their homes to minorities. However, one neighbor decided to break the covenant and sold his home to the Shelleys. When white residents found out that a black family intended to move in, they filed a lawsuit in an effort to prevent them from doing so.

At the first trial, the court ruled in favor of the Shelleys, but the lawyer of the family who was suing them, the Kraemers, took the case before the Supreme Court of Missouri. That court sided with the Kraemers, saying that the covenant was legal because it was a private agreement.

When Marshall brought the case before the Supreme Court, he won a unanimous decision. The six justices who voted (three did not) all agreed that courts could not stop real estate sales to African Americans on the basis of their race, even if the property was covered by racially restricted covenants. The decision stated, in part, that:

> The historical context in which the Fourteenth Amendment became a part of the Constitution should not be forgotten. Whatever else the framers sought to achieve, it is clear that the matter of primary concern was the establishment of equality in the enjoyment of basic civil and political rights and the preservation of those rights from discriminatory action on the part of the States based on considerations of race or color. Seventy-five years ago this Court announced that the provisions of the Amendment are to be construed with this fundamental purpose in mind. Upon full consideration, we have concluded that in these cases the States have acted to deny petitioners the equal protection of the laws guaranteed by the Fourteenth Amendment.

Shelley v. Kraemer did not make racially restrictive covenants illegal, but it did become a major milestone in the fight for equality.

1950: *McLaurin v. Oklahoma State Regents for Higher Education*

McLaurin v. Oklahoma State Regents for Higher Education was the case that damaged *Plessy v. Ferguson* the most and set it up to be shot down. George McLaurin wasn't a child, but a sixty-one-year-old man, who already had a master's degree and a teaching job. He wanted a doctorate, or PhD, in school administration, so he applied to the University of Oklahoma College of Education. Knowing the law under the Gaines decision, the school did not want to have to provide separate schools or programs for McLaurin or other African-American graduate students. So they said McLaurin could attend, but once he arrived, he was always segregated into separate parts of the classroom, library, cafeteria, and restrooms. Sometimes he had to attend classes by himself; other times, he was given a desk that was roped off or otherwise physically separated from the white students. Marshall argued in front of the Supreme Court that this was humiliating treatment, in direct violation of the Fourteenth Amendment. In 1950, the Supreme Court agreed. They ruled that universities must provide the same treatment for African-American students as they do for other races.

1954: *Brown v. Board of Education of Topeka, Kansas*

Brown v. Board of Education of Topeka, Kansas has been called the greatest court case of Thurgood Marshall's career, and more than sixty years later, it's easy to see why.

This consolidated case is named after one case: *Oliver Brown versus the Board of Education of Topeka, Kansas*, usually abbreviated to *Brown v. Board of Education*. But, in fact, it represents five combined cases. Marshall and the rest of the LDF wanted to build a case that challenged segregation with several **plaintiffs**, in case one or two decided to drop out. This would mean that the case could continue even if several plaintiffs no longer wanted to be involved. The LDF

G. W. McLaurin
was forced to sit
separately from his
white classmates at the
University of Oklahoma.

knew that this was an incredibly important case: they needed to make it clear to the nine white justices, and prove conclusively, that segregated schools were harmful to children and that segregation was unconstitutional. The five cases that made up this important case are *Briggs v. Elliott, Gebhart v. Belton, Bolling v. Sharpe, Davis v. School Board of Prince Edward County, Virginia*, and, of course, *Brown v. Board of Education of Topeka, Kansas*.

Briggs v. Elliot

One of the five cases was *Briggs v. Elliot*, which was originally tried in Clarendon County, South Carolina. Harry and Liza Briggs, African-American parents, sued the state because they saw the condition of the schools their children were forced to go to as inadequate compared to the schools for white children.

The LDF team noted the blatant contrasts in the schools. Those for African-American children were only in session for about six months out of the year, with the reason being that the children were expected to be working in the fields during planting and harvest seasons. Classes were often composed of fifty or more children, there were often only one or two teachers to serve the entire school, and the buildings could be described as shacks or cabins, which usually had leaky roofs along with no running water, indoor bathrooms, or heat. The children often sat on benches, holding their books and papers on their laps, and their textbooks were usually old and outdated.

The schools for white children ran on a more normal schedule—nine months out of the year—and the well-constructed school buildings had heat, water, and restrooms. With classes of only twenty to twenty-five students and one teacher per classroom, the children sat at desks and studied from new books. There was more proof in the numbers: the county spent $43 a year for each black student and $180 a year—more than three times as much—for each white student. The LDF also discovered that the teachers in the white schools were being paid much higher salaries than the teachers working at the African-American schools.

The governor of South Carolina heard about the case and decided to try to prevent it from going before the Supreme Court. He quickly allotted funding to repair the African-American schools, raise their teachers' salaries, and buy the same books and other supplies. Marshall changed his strategy. Instead of arguing that the schools were separate but not equal, he challenged South Carolina to end segregation entirely. He quoted Charles Hamilton Houston and said, "There is no such thing as separate-but-equal. Segregation itself imports inequality."

The strategy worked. Marshall deliberately lost the case at the state level. He then presented the case to the Supreme Court, who decided they would not hear it. That was when Marshall instituted Plan B: combining the Briggs case with the four others.

Gebhart v. Belton

Two more cases the NAACP took on were *Bulah v. Gebhart* and *Belton v. Gebhart*, both out of Delaware. They were consolidated into *Gebhart v. Belton*. An African-American mother, Sarah Bulah, sued the Delaware Department of Public Instruction after they refused to provide her daughter, Shirley, with a bus to her school, which was 2 miles (3.2 km) away. In a nearby town, Claymont, a mother named Ethel Belton sued after the school board refused to make improvements at her daughter's school. Her daughter attended Howard High School, which was 20 miles (32 km) from her home, had three times as many students as the white high school in town, and had hardly any extracurricular activities.

Bolling v. Sharpe

The Bolling case was different from the others for four reasons. First, the Fourteenth Amendment's equal protection clause only applied

THE DOLL EXPERIMENT

A study by psychologist Kenneth Clark helped to shape Marshall's arguments in *Brown v. Board of Education*. Because of Dr. Clark's research, Marshall was ready to argue that systematic segregation and racism were harmful to African-American children because it kept them from reaching their full potential—not only in school but in later life, when they became adults and tried to find jobs.

In his studies, Dr. Clark performed a famous experiment. First, he showed four dolls to groups of black children between the ages of three and seven. The dolls were all identical except for their skin color, and Dr. Clark asked the children which dolls they liked best. He was disturbed to discover that most of them chose the white-skinned dolls and said that the other dolls were ugly or looked "bad." They described the white dolls as looking "nice" or pretty. Yet, when he asked them which dolls were most like them, they chose the dark-skinned dolls. One boy even used a racial slur to describe the doll he said looked most like him. Clark concluded that African-American children had poor self-images as a result of segregation.

Although Dr. Clark's research had been conducted years earlier, mostly in support of his wife's work toward her master's degree thesis, Marshall brought him before the Supreme Court to testify as an expert.

to state laws, and the District of Columbia, where this case began, was legislated under a federal law that mandated segregated schools in the District.

Second, even though the all-black schools the plaintiffs were forced to attend were vastly inferior to the all-white schools, the lawyers did not initially present evidence of inequality. They simply said that the principle of "separate but equal" was unconstitutional, even if the separate facilities were of equal quality.

Third, this was not an NAACP case. A parent named Gardner Bishop had approached Charles Hamilton Houston to take the case after he had unsuccessfully petitioned to have his children and several others admitted to a brand-new segregated junior high school. Houston was preparing for the case when he was stricken with a heart attack. He asked a colleague, James Nabrit Jr., to take over. Nabrit, who worked for the NAACP, filed the case in US District Court, where his arguments were shot down. He was preparing an appeal when the US Supreme Court asked to review the details and combined it with the other cases that became *Brown v. Board of Education*.

Finally, the ruling in this case was decided under the Due Process Clause of the Fifth Amendment instead of the Fourteenth Amendment Equal Protection Clause.

Davis v. School Board of Prince Edward County, Virginia

In another case, *Davis v. School Board of Prince Edward County, Virginia*, the black students themselves went on strike. They were fed up with attending an overcrowded, rundown school built for 180 students that had 450 enrolled. After two weeks of the strike, 117 students asked the school board to banish segregation in the schools of their county. The school board refused, and one of the students, Barbara Rose Johns, wrote to the NAACP, who took on the case. The parents of Dorothy Davis, a ninth-grader, allowed their last name to be the leading one on the paperwork.

Finally, there was the single case from which the combined cases got their name. Linda Brown was a third-grader whose parents objected to the fact that she had to walk six blocks and cross railroad tracks to get picked up by a bus that took her to her school. One day, her father, Reverend Oliver Brown, brought her into Sumner Elementary School, which was within walking distance of their home. He asked the principal if Linda could enroll there since it was so much closer. The principal refused. Reverend Brown contacted the NAACP and asked for their help in suing the school system, which they gladly gave. Of course, the Board of Education of Topeka, just like the other school boards and school districts mentioned here, claimed that what they were doing was legal because of the separate but equal doctrine.

These five cases were what the NAACP had been waiting for. They wanted to go after *Plessy v. Ferguson*, once and for all.

When Marshall first stepped in front of the court in December 1952 to argue the case, he made a compelling argument. He came right out and stated that segregation in schools had to end. He said it created a cycle of poverty and ignorance because an inadequate education put African-American students at a disadvantage where they couldn't get ahead. He not only pointed out that the schools and the money spent on them were unequal, but he declared that there was a worse problem: there was research proving that African-American children suffered emotional harm such as low self-worth due to being segregated. He discussed the findings of Dr. Kenneth Clark, a psychologist and professor who taught at City College of New York, which backed his assertion. In his closing remarks, he said, "There is nothing involved in this case other than race and color."

By the time Marshall and the opposing attorney, John Davis, had finished presenting their sides of the argument, it was June 1953, six months after the case began. The justices announced that they wanted to set the case aside for a time, so both sides would have time to think about the true meaning of the Fourteenth Amendment. They wanted to consider the intentions of the people who had created the amendment, and whether they meant for segregation to exist forever. Marshall didn't know if he had convinced a majority of the judges. He needed five of the nine to agree with him. Then, something unexpected happened: Chief Justice Fred Vinson had a heart attack and died. The case could not resume until a new chief justice had been appointed. Two months later, Earl Warren took on the role, and the case resumed.

Marshall summed up his case yet again. He said he had studied the Fourteenth Amendment closely during the **hiatus**, and that he was more convinced than ever that it was designed to protect all citizens of the United States, regardless of color. He said there was no reason to believe that African Americans were inferior to whites, and he told the judges that if they thought segregation should continue, they should have to prove that such an inferiority existed. He ended by saying that school segregation would ensure that the black citizens of the United States would never be able to improve themselves, and that such a situation was exactly the opposite of what the Fourteenth Amendment stated.

Davis also stuck to the argument that he had put forth from the beginning: that segregation, and the separate but equal policy, had been the law for a long time, and that there was really no reason to change it. He warned that forcing integration would upset people and probably lead to violence; he seemed to say that keeping African-American students segregated was really for their own safety. What the whole case would boil down to was what the Supreme Court justices believed. Once again, the justices announced that they wanted to take a few months to discuss the issue.

As it turns out, Chief Justice Warren agreed with Marshall, although he couldn't say it publicly at the time. He believed that segregation had to be abolished. However, he wanted all nine of the justices to agree on their decision. He didn't want it to be known that some of them did not agree; he wanted the country's citizens to know that the Supreme Court was in complete agreement, a unified force in this monumental decision.

Finally, in May 1954, the Supreme Court announced that it had made its decision. Marshall was actually out of town, down in Mobile, Alabama, when he got the call saying it was time to return the Washington, DC. He rushed onto the next flight out to the nation's capital and took his place before the court. Chief Justice Warren announced the verdict: in a unanimous decision, the Supreme Court ruled that segregation was illegal, and that separate educational facilities at all levels were inherently unequal and a violation of the equal protection clause of the Fourteenth Amendment. Marshall and the NAACP had finally been successful in knocking down *Plessy v. Ferguson* and the Jim Crow laws. He later said, "I was so happy, I was numb."

Part of the text of the Supreme Court's ruling stated:

> Today, education is perhaps the most important function of state and local governments. **Compulsory** school attendance laws and the great expenditures for education both demonstrate our recognition of the importance of education to our democratic society ... It is the very foundation of good citizenship. Today it is a principal instrument in awakening the child to cultural values, in preparing him for later professional training, and in helping him to adjust normally to his environment. In these days, it is doubtful that any child may reasonably be expected to succeed in life if he is denied the opportunity of an education. Such an opportunity, where the state has undertaken to provide it, is a right which must be made available to all on equal terms.

Marshall must have been particularly happy with the following language, which strongly supported his argument:

We come then to the question presented: Does segregation of children in public schools solely on the basis of race, even though the physical facilities and other "tangible" factors may be equal, deprive the children of the minority group of equal educational opportunities? We believe that it does.

After the lawyers were excused from the courtroom, Marshall stopped to answer reporters' questions for a few minutes before calling his staff in New York City. He wanted to be the one to announce the good news to them. Later, he posed for pictures on the front steps of the Supreme Court building with his co-counsel before flying back to New York to celebrate with the rest of the NAACP. One report of the day, though, tells a charming story: after stepping away from the reporters, Marshall let down his guard. He swooped up a little white boy named Bill Greenhill, the son of a colleague who just happened to be in town visiting that day. He put Bill on his shoulders and went running through the marble halls with glee. It must have been quite a sight to see.

Excitement didn't quite rule the day. Even after champagne toasts with his colleagues and friends and a celebratory dinner back in New York, Marshall said something that meant he must have somehow known what was to come. When another member of the party implied that the work of the NAACP was now done, Marshall shook his head. "I don't want any of you to fool yourselves; it's just begun, the fight has just begun."

CHAPTER FIVE

Life Goes On

Many people still consider *Brown v. Board of Education* to be the single most important Supreme Court decision of the past one hundred years. It did more than overturn segregation in the country's schools: this case was a defining moment for the civil rights movement, and it was arguably the movement's greatest legal triumph. It reversed decades of racist laws and helped to bring down a racial hierarchy that existed in the United States. It addressed the post–Civil War mentality that allowed for vigilante justice and lynchings perpetrated against an entire race of people. It forever changed American society by giving African Americans the facilities, accommodations, and jobs they deserved. It led to the social movement that generated the 1964 Civil Rights Act, which in turn begat political and economic changes that eventually contributed to the rise of successful African Americans like media mogul Oprah Winfrey, American Express CEO Ken Chennault, and President Barack Obama.

In 1957, Thurgood Marshall was working as an attorney for the NAACP.

It was also a personal and professional triumph for Thurgood Marshall, who had spent his entire legal career fighting for the rights of the African American community, little by little, case by case. After all, Charles Hamilton Houston had been mentoring him and leading him to that momentous court decision for two decades.

Going after segregation in education must have seemed like an incredibly daunting task back then. At the time Marshall took the *Brown v. Board of Education* case to court, seventeen states, along with the District of Columbia, actually required their public schools to be racially segregated. Four more states—Arizona, Kansas, New Mexico, and Wyoming—let local communities set their own similar laws. To convince nine white judges to overturn a network of state laws and a nationwide mentality was an enormous achievement. The *Brown* decision was not just an argument against the idea of "separate but equal," it was a fight against the country's desire for the status quo. Black students were not only segregated from white students but completely denied meaningful educational opportunities.

But Marshall had little time to rest on his laurels after the Supreme Court awarded him the victory. First, there was the matter of his wife Vivian's health. After she passed away and he returned from his vacation and his mourning period, he discovered that he had been right: desegregation was not happening quickly, smoothly, or easily. He had predicted that it would take around ten years for desegregation to happen in all of the United States' public schools. It actually took longer.

Despite the fact that the Supreme Court's decisions are the highest judicial rulings in the United States, many state and local governments decided to ignore their ruling. Segregation, as John Davis had said in his arguments before the court, had been the law of the land for generations, and many people didn't see why it had to end. Especially in the South, where slavery and the accompanying belief that African Americans were inferior beings had been ingrained in people for generations, change was slow in coming.

Political Resistance

Almost as soon as the decision was announced, some politicians spoke up against the Supreme Court and what they had done. Senator Richard Russell of Georgia, who was the leader of the Southern Democrats in the Senate, complained that the court's decision was "a flagrant abuse of judicial power." He said that issues like segregation should be decided by lawmakers, not by the courts.

Senator Marion Price Daniel, a Democrat from Texas, called the verdict "disappointing" and said he didn't understand why the court had ruled as it did. Governor William B. Umstead of North Carolina also said, in a statement released by his office, that he was "terribly disappointed" in the Supreme Court's ruling.

Another Southern senator, Allen J. Ellender from Louisiana, was a little more polite: "I am of course very much disappointed by this. But I don't want to criticize the Supreme Court. It is bound to have a very great effect until we readjust ourselves to it." He added that he felt there would be "violent repercussions" if enforcement were ordered too quickly.

Representative John Bell Williams, a Democrat from Mississippi, called the date of the Supreme Court's decision "Black Monday." Later, a group called the White Citizens' Council formed in Mississippi, led by a circuit court judge named Thomas Pickens Brady. They borrowed Williams's term for the title of their handbook, *Black Monday*, which laid out their philosophy. They said that the NAACP should be **nullified**, that the government should create a separate state for Negroes, and that public schools should be abolished—because private schools wouldn't be subject to the *Brown v. Board of Education* ruling.

Georgia's governor, Herman Talmadge, went so far as to declare that the Supreme Court had "reduced our Constitution to a mere scrap of paper" and vowed that his state would not accept or abide by the court's decision.

North Carolina's state legislature passed a law saying that local school boards were responsible for enforcing integration. That way, every time a school refused to integrate, parents would have to sue the school board, and these individual lawsuits slowed down the process considerably.

In 1956, a group of senators and representatives from nine Southern states sent what was called the "Southern Manifesto" to the Supreme Court, telling the justices that not only would they not accept the ruling, but they would fight to keep from desegregating their schools. They said they would close public schools to keep white children from having to mix with African-American children.

This actually happened in Prince Edward County, Virginia, one of the school districts whose lawsuit had been an important component of the *Brown v. Board of Education* challenge. Officials there closed the public schools for five years rather than have to integrate them. Some African-American students had to move in with relatives or friends in other counties so they could continue their educations, but some never finished school because of the actions of school leaders.

Even governors and other lawmakers who believed in the correctness of the court's decision in *Brown v. Board of Education* hesitated to act—especially in the South. They were afraid to push too hard for fear of **alienating** their voters. They suspected that protests and violence would erupt, and they were right. To be fair, some state governors did announce that they would follow the law, even if they didn't agree with the Supreme Court's ruling.

The Southern media seemed to reflect both sides of the argument. In Richmond, Virginia, an article in a newspaper contained the following quote: "We accept the Supreme Court's ruling. We do not accept it willingly, or cheerfully or philosophically. We accept it because we have to." Conversely, a piece in the *News & Observer* in Raleigh, North Carolina, stated that "[the ruling] will be met in the South with the good sense and the good will of the people of both races in a manner which will serve the children and honor America."

Senator Strom Thurmond
of South Carolina was
an outspoken foe of
desegregation.

Finally, the main paper in Greenville, Mississippi, published a piece that announced, "If ever a region asked for such a decree, the South did through its shocking calculated and cynical disobedience to its own state constitutions, which specify that separate school systems must be equal."

Unfortunately, many citizens of the United States took their cues from their elected leaders. "Massive resistance" was the name given the movement to delay desegregation in the schools and elsewhere. On the citizens' level, rocks, bricks, and worse were thrown through the windows of African-American families' homes, with notes attached threatening them not to send their children to white schools. African-American parents lost their jobs, were turned down for loans, and had their businesses boycotted. School systems

US deputy marshals had to escort six-year-old Ruby Bridges to and from her elementary school in New Orleans, Louisiana.

still refused to let black children enroll, and law enforcement did nothing. Lawmakers and politicians looked the other way. Nobody seemed to care that they were in violation of the federal government.

Actions, Not Words

Integration went more smoothly in some schools than in others, even in the South. In 1956, Clinton High School in Clinton, Tennessee, was supposed to be the first Southern high school to be integrated after the *Brown* decision. The citizens and the school system thought they were ready, and the process was moving along smoothly. Then John Kasper arrived in town. Kasper was the leader of the White Citizens' Council, and he was a staunch segregationist. He stirred up other people who were against desegregation, inciting protests and riots for weeks. However, when the day came, several white citizens escorted the African-American students to class. One of these escorts was badly beaten by angry protesters, and the school closed temporarily, but it reopened six days later.

In North Carolina, four students attempting to be the first African-American children to attend the previously all-white Harding High School in Charlotte were greeted by angry white mobs. The protesters screamed obscenities and racial slurs at the students. One girl's family feared so deeply for her safety that they withdrew her from Harding and sent her out of state to attend high school elsewhere.

In 1956, a US District Court judge ordered the desegregation of the New Orleans, Louisiana, public schools. It took until 1960 for legal protests and appeals to be settled. The judge finally laid out a plan that required the schools to integrate one grade per year, beginning with the first grade. The school board chose the best candidates based on their performance on a test, and out of the six children they chose, four agreed to give integration a try. Six-year-old Ruby Bridges walked into a public school to integrate it, escorted by US marshals, and in response, white parents withdrew all of her classmates. Ruby completed that school year alone with the support of her teachers and a child psychiatrist.

In Marshall's hometown of Baltimore, Maryland, integration problems were fairly mild. The city opened the white schools to black

WHATEVER HAPPENED TO THE LITTLE ROCK NINE?

The nine students who desegregated Central High School did not just happen to go to that school. They were chosen by Daisy Bates, the president of the Arkansas NAACP. Bates considered carefully which students possessed the strength and determination to face the negative reactions she knew they would encounter. She prepared them with intensive counseling sessions that included lessons in how to respond to hostile situations.

Bates drove eight of the nine students to school on that first day. The ninth student, Elizabeth Eckford, did not have a phone in her house, so Bates was unable to reach her to tell her of the plan. The picture of Eckford walking up to the school alone, surrounded by screaming, hostile white people, is one of the most famous images in history.

Of those nine students, only one graduated from Central High: Ernest Green, who was the only senior that first year. The following year, Governor Faubus ordered the schools to close so they wouldn't have to desegregate. Seven of the nine either had to earn their diplomas through **correspondence courses** or they had to move to other towns (sometimes in other states) to attend school and graduate. One girl, Minnijean Brown, got expelled that first year for retaliating against the almost-daily abuse she faced. She moved to New York City to live with Dr. Kenneth Clark and his wife, graduated from a private school, and eventually became a social activist.

enrollment, and many white people protested. Some fights broke out in the streets. Nearby, in the northern half of Virginia, desegregation happened fairly peacefully. However, in the southern half of the state, Governor Thomas Stanley backed the citizens who put up a fight. He proudly stated, "I shall use every legal means necessary to continue segregated schools in Virginia."

The governor of Arkansas, Orval Faubus, went even further than Governor Stanley. In 1957, citizens of Little Rock protested the integration of their schools by blocking nine African-American students from entering an all-white high school. Faubus not only supported the protesters, but he sent the state National Guard to help them bar the doors. He even openly declared that "blood would run in the streets" if black students attempted to enter the school. President Eisenhower had to step in. He ordered the US Army to send troops to Little Rock to help the students. Members of the 101st Airborne Division had to line up alongside the nine children to protect them as they finally filed into school, and they stayed for the remainder of the year to ensure the students' safety. They escorted the Little Rock Nine, as the media dubbed the students, to and from school every day and stood guard in the hallways during classes.

Undeterred, Governor Faubus tried another tactic. At the end of the school year, he announced that he was closing all public schools for a year. He claimed that they couldn't be integrated without fear of more violence. Marshall went back to the Supreme Court and argued the case of the Little Rock Nine, formally called *Cooper v. Aaron*. He stated:

> Even if it be claimed that tension will result which will disturb the educational process, this is preferable to the complete breakdown of education which will result from teaching that courts of law will bow to violence … It's only a question of time until integration is completed. We'll solve the problem peacefully—and gradually.

Soldiers from the 101st Airborne Division protected the Little Rock Nine at the all-white Central High School in Little Rock, Arkansas.

Needless to say, the Supreme Court ruled that closing the schools to avoid integration was against the law, and the schools reopened. The court also reminded the governor and legislature of Arkansas that their interpretation of the Constitution was the "supreme law of the land" and that state and local governments were bound to the Supreme Court's decisions and not allowed to annul them with legislation, amendments, or orders. As one writer put it, *Brown v. Board of Education* provided the foundation for school integration in the 1950s and 1960s, and *Cooper v. Aaron* provided the muscle.

Marshall did not like the stories he was hearing from other communities around the country. In his role as head of the LDF, he urged the Supreme Court to set a timeline and rules for desegregation. They did not do exactly what he asked, and only announced that segregated schools should make a "prompt and reasonable start toward full compliance." Instead of a timeline, they said that schools should proceed with "all deliberate speed." This gave the resistant school systems the ability to drag their feet. By 1962, the military again had to intervene to help the cause of desegregation along.

That year, a black student named James Meredith applied to attend college at the University of Mississippi. He was a resident of the state and was trying to exercise his right to attend the school, but the university hadn't followed the law laid down by *Brown v. Board of Education*. They were still a whites-only institution. Meredith sued the university for discrimination and lost at the state level but won his appeal to have his case heard before the Supreme Court. They, of course, ruled in his favor. When he attempted to register for classes, though, angry mobs of white people blocked the door. Riots broke out, and two people were killed before Attorney General Robert Kennedy sent five hundred US marshals to end the violence. President John F. Kennedy followed up on his brother's actions by sending military police, troops from the Mississippi National Guard, and officials from the US Border Patrol. On October 1, 1962, James Meredith finally became the first black student to enroll at the

Chief US Marshal James McShane (*left*) and Assistant Attorney General for Civil Rights John Doar (*right*) flank James Meredith as he forces integration at the University of Mississippi.

University of Mississippi. He graduated to become a lawyer and civil rights activist who also participated in politics.

It wasn't until the late 1960s and early 1970s that the Supreme Court finally gave Marshall what he'd asked for in the mid-1950s. Desegregation, which was supposed to be proceeding "with all deliberate speed," was happening far too slowly. Marshall was forced to lead the LDF in suing hundreds of school districts across the country for their refusal to integrate. It wasn't until after he had joined the court that two cases, *Green v. County School Board* and *Swann v. Charlotte-Mecklenburg*, caused the Supreme Court to order that segregated systems must be dismantled "root and branch." They meant that any and all segregated policies must be abolished, including anything that had to do with classrooms, faculty, school system staff, extracurricular activities, and the transportation that took the kids to and from school. They issued detailed orders on how school systems must go about desegregating. This nearly eliminated the lawsuits that were clogging the lower courts and slowing down the process.

It took until 1972 for the majority of Southern schools, about 90 percent, to be officially integrated. Schools didn't necessarily have racially balanced student bodies, however. Because black children and white children attended schools closest to their homes, and because neighborhoods were still segregated, school enrollments didn't always reflect the changes. The laws, however, were on the books.

The Ripple Effect

The Supreme Court's decision in *Brown v. Board of Education* would positively affect many other areas in the lives of African Americans. Marshall and the rest of the NAACP had always known that if they could figure out how to end segregation in the schools, they could use that as leverage to abolish segregation elsewhere. For years after that landmark decision, they used the language of the Supreme Court's decision to win further victories.

For example, there were segregation-based laws that enforced separation of the races everywhere from hospitals to circuses. People could be fined or even jailed for printing or distributing publications that contained language in favor of interracial marriage. Some of these laws were ridiculous in their extremes, such as in those states that had laws against textbooks for white children being stored in the same place as those used by black children.

Brown v. Board of Education also helped advance civil rights legislation in 1957, 1960, 1964, 1965, and 1968 that ended legal support for status based on race. By 1963, the NAACP had been instrumental in striking down laws that allowed segregation in public buildings, including places of recreation; on transportation; in restaurants; and in housing—just as they had set out to do.

Because of the publicity that had surrounded the case from the beginning, and especially its dramatic conclusion, people all across the country knew about it and realized what it meant. Both blacks and whites were energized and inspired to fight together for civil rights. They were encouraged to desegregate interstate transportation through freedom rides and local buses and other public facilities by supporting Rosa Parks. They challenged the status quo with peaceful activities like sit-ins, and put their lives in danger to help register African Americans in the Deep South to vote. They stood up to people who tried to bar the admission of African Americans to southern universities.

The silver lining to the persecution of the Little Rock Nine, as Marshall himself said, was that people who believed in integration would know what lengths the government would go to in order to help them. He said, "In some states—where people wanted to integrate but were afraid of trouble—they may go ahead now that they see they really have the backing of the federal government."

By declaring that the discriminatory nature of racial segregation "violates the Fourteenth Amendment to the US Constitution, which guarantees all citizens equal protection of the laws," *Brown v. Board of Education* also helped to shape national and international policies regarding human rights. The case received media attention all over the world, including in French West Africa (now Senegal), India, and Australia. *Brown v. Board of Education* has had a lasting global impact because it affected the interpretation of law in countries all over the world. For example, the people of South Africa used it as a legal and moral precedent when fighting for their own equal rights after decades of segregation under **apartheid**.

Because of what Marshall and *Brown v. Board of Education* were able to accomplish for the African-American civil rights movement, its results also inspired and influenced social movements such as women's rights and women's liberation, the LGBT movement, and accommodations for people with disabilities. Court cases and laws that promote equality for these groups were hung on the framework of *Brown v. Board of Education*.

It even helped improve international relations between the United States and other countries. It showed people of other nations that American democracy was changing for the better. Before then, the civil rights problems in the United States had long been a topic for editorials around the world. It was hard to explain why or how, in a country that was supposed to be an example of democracy, citizens were segregated by race, and some of them were brutalized for trying to exercise their basic rights.

In the aftermath of the case, though, not everything was positive. Many of the plaintiffs lost their jobs or had difficulty securing loans in retaliation for their participation. Even members of their families suffered similar punishments. In Topeka, Kansas, the hometown of Linda Brown, desegregation had begun even before the case was brought before the Supreme Court. However, it hurt the black community when many teachers lost their jobs as the all-black schools were closed. In fact, this happened all over the country. Worst of all, in South Carolina, white people burned down the house and church of one of the better-known plaintiffs in the *Briggs v. Elliott* case, the Reverend Joseph A. DeLaine. Reverend DeLaine also reported that gunshots had been fired at him one night. He ended up leaving the state in fear for his personal safety. Even Judge J. Waties Waring, the white judge who had written the dissenting opinion in the original case, faced death threats and other intimidation after his involvement. He ended up retiring from the bench in 1952 and moving to New York City.

Perhaps the saddest footnote to the case involves Linda Brown, the little third-grade girl whose name is part of the famous ruling. Unbelievably, Topeka did not formulate a workable desegregation plan for its schools until 1994. Linda never got to go to the all-white school down the street. When she grew up and got married, her children attended segregated public schools. Based on her own experience, the court's ruling had not been fulfilled.

Celebrity Lawyer

Marshall did enjoy a certain amount of notoriety in the wake of the court's decision. He was interviewed for radio and television as well as print media, and he traveled the country making speeches. He even appeared on the cover of *Time* magazine that summer.

Knowing how the effects of a Supreme Court decision could spread, he said that African-Americans had now been given the foundation for wiping out segregation, not only in the schools but in other areas of society as well. He said he was sure that someday soon, there would be no more "whites only" stores, restaurants, performance venues, and bathrooms. He reminded people that African Americans should be able to enjoy the same freedoms, privileges, and luxuries as anyone else and called race and color "irrelevant."

In the 1960s, Marshall's methods began to be perceived differently as the civil rights movement started to take off. As much as he believed in equality, his fame began to be eclipsed, for the moment, by other civil rights leaders who were taking to the streets. Then, in 1961, he faced the Supreme Court for the last time in a case for the NAACP, *Garner v. Louisiana*. Two African-American college students had been arrested and fined for participating in a sit-in at a whites-only lunch counter in Baton Rouge, Louisiana. They had been charged with disturbing the peace. Marshall didn't like that they had broken the law, but he did believe in protecting the rights of individuals, so he appealed the conviction on their behalf. He won, and in yet another unanimous ruling, the Supreme Court overturned the boys' conviction. The case set an important precedent and was a huge victory for the sit-in movement. The Supreme Court said that the police could not reasonably foresee that the boys' peaceful protest might cause a disturbance. After that, Thurgood Marshall was on to bigger and better things, thanks to Presidents John F. Kennedy and Lyndon B. Johnson.

CHAPTER SIX

Brown v. Board of Education *Today*

There is no question that Thurgood Marshall's accomplishment in winning *Brown v. Board of Education* is relevant today. Lawyers still study his arguments during the case, as well as his later writings about it. His words in the courtroom are still quoted and expanded upon today.

African-American children grow up learning that one of their own fought for their right to education. He also serves as a perfect example of what education can help a person accomplish in life. Marshall wasn't born into a life of privilege, but he was able to create one for himself and for his children.

However, in recent years, the impact of *Brown v. Board of Education* has come under some critical scrutiny. While it was certainly a landmark case for its time, in the long run, has it

The first African-American president of the United States, Barack Obama was also voted the first African-American president of the *Harvard Law Review* in 1990.

done what it was supposed to do? Are the ideals that it supported still being seen today? Several civil rights experts have tackled these questions and more, only to discover that the effects of *Brown* have indeed changed over time. In 2016, as this book goes to press, where does America's educational system stand in relation to this ruling?

First, the good news. There are two generations of United States citizens who don't know what it's like to grow up in a segregated society. They have always gone to school with people of other races. People may still use terms like "us" and "them," but in this country, people of all races, colors, religions, and national origins live, work, and play together.

Also, since 1954, thousands of African Americans have graduated from high school, college or university, law school, medical school, and dental school. To be more specific, before *Brown*, only about one in seven African Americans earned a high school degree. Today, nearly 85 percent of African-American adults have one. As for college degrees, prior to 1954, only about one in forty black people earned them. Now, more than one in five hold one, and many of them have used their educations to make valuable contributions in almost every field.

From 2009 to 2017, a young African-American lawyer and senator from Illinois served as the president of the United States. His wife, the First Lady, was equally accomplished and educated. Barack and Michelle Obama probably owe their ascendance in American politics to Thurgood Marshall and *Brown v. Board of Education*.

Various Opinions

Brown obviously did not succeed in completely abolishing school segregation. In New York City today, for instance, more than half of the public schools have student bodies that are at least 90 percent black and Hispanic. In Alabama, nearly a quarter of black students attend a school with white enrollment of 1 percent or less.

The Supreme Court's official decision in *Brown v. Board of Education.*

Many civil rights experts have been discussing what they call a "resegregation" trend.

In spring 2004, as *Brown v. Board of Education* turned fifty, Columbia Law School asked two alumni, both civil rights experts, to give their opinions on the case. Jack Greenberg, who was still teaching law at Columbia at the time, was actually a member of Thurgood Marshall's legal team that worked on *Brown*. Lino Graglia is a law professor at the University of Texas at Austin.

Perhaps not surprisingly, Greenberg feels that *Brown v. Board of Education* produced many positive effects. He points out that first and foremost, it corrected the nation's morality on the subject of segregation. He considers it a critical force in launching the civil rights movement, which then led to the Civil Rights Acts of the mid-1960s. He points out that in the years following the *Brown* decision, the number of black congressmen went from two to forty. Major corporations like Time Warner, Merrill Lynch, and Xerox had black CEOs. In 1954, some states only had a single black lawyer; in 2004, there were ten thousand black law students. In other words, the decision affected more than just schools and schoolchildren: It had an effect on African-American society as a whole.

Graglia was a bit more critical of its effects, especially considering the court's lack of attempts to enforce the decision on their own. He felt it was wrong that resistant states ignored the law or decided to respond to it by simply ending free public education. As he put it, "the 1955 *Brown* decision … held that the states did not have to end segregation until it was 'practicable' to do so, which in the Deep South meant never."

He believes that racial segregation in Southern schools ended not after *Brown* but as a result of the 1964 Civil Rights Act. Graglia says the Act "ratified and made effective what Congress and everyone else thought was the *Brown* principle: a prohibition of all official race discrimination."

Graglia also criticized the decision for changing the way people—from lawyers to citizens—think of the role of the Supreme

Court. He believes that the Supreme Court justices overstepped their bounds by making their decisions based on social policy, not on the Constitution. He called it a "perversion of the system of government created by the Constitution, the basic principles of which are self-government through elected representatives, decentralized power (federalism), and separation of powers." He blames the *Brown* case for creating "government by majority vote of a committee of nine unelected, life-tenured lawyers making the most basic policy decisions for the nation as a whole from Washington, D.C."

As for whether public schools in America were still segregated—although not by law—in 2004, Greenberg opined that modern school segregation is mostly the result of residential segregation, saying that black children living in the inner cities don't have access to white suburban schools. He admits that there is no easy solution to this problem. Graglia says that it is compulsory integration that actually violates *Brown*'s banning of official race discrimination. He feels that areas of residential race concentration are normal, whether for social, economic, or other reasons, and that attempting to make schools racially balanced is both counterproductive and pointless.

In 2009, Stanford University released the results of a study that took a comprehensive look at whether court-ordered **busing** was important to integration in public education. The study showed that "districts that stopped forcing schools to mix students by race have seen a gradual but steady—and significant—return of racial isolation, especially at the elementary level."

By the time the sixtieth anniversary of *Brown* rolled around, another expert weighed in with his opinions, saying that this landmark decision has lost its relevance in the twenty-first century. Richard Rothstein, an educational analyst, declared that *Brown* has been unsuccessful in its mission because it is still unfulfilled. He says that school segregation persists in American public education today.

Rothstein points out that school integration gains following *Brown* have stalled, and he claims that black children are more racially and socioeconomically isolated today than at any time since

1970. He says there are too many other policies that need to be in place to support true equality in schools.

His most important point is that resource equality on its own is insufficient. In 1954, schools for black children had resource shortages. Today, school inequalities are nowhere near as unbalanced as they once were, but Rothstein points out that disadvantaged students require greater resources, not the same ones as middle-class white students, to achieve success in school.

In Rothstein's opinion, to narrow the achievement gap between minority and white children, these resources would include high-quality early childhood programs; comprehensive after-school and summer programs; full-service school health clinics; more skilled teachers; and smaller classes.

Rothstein gives a lot of weight to the importance of early childhood programs, designed to work with children from birth to school age. He says that research has proven "that the most important predictor for young children of later academic success is the general background knowledge with which they come to school." White middle- and upper-class children tend to have more educated parents who read to them often and expose them to various enrichment activities, from trips to the zoo to visits to the library and even travel to other cities and countries. Children from lower-income families tend to have less-educated parents with lower literacy levels; they are not read to frequently or given as many educational learning experiences, nor do they tend to travel for leisure. Rothstein says schools need a way to shrink the difference between the school readiness of lower-income children and that of middle-class children. Older students from lower-income families, in middle school and high school, need to be able to participate in field trips; club activities; music, art, and dance classes; and organized athletics comparable to what the average middle-class child gets.

Rothstein also says that because children from segregated neighborhoods tend to see and experience more crime and violence, they need more support services that they usually don't get, like school counselors and school social workers. Racially segregated neighborhoods tend to have fewer physicians practicing in them, so children living in those neighborhoods usually receive less routine health care, not to mention preventive care. They tend to have unique medical problems, like iron-deficiency anemia and lead poisoning, or common health issues like asthma, from living in less-healthy environments. Kids in these neighborhoods might not be identified as having trouble with their vision, their hearing, or even their teeth until they get to elementary school, by which point they have already fallen behind. Rothstein says that putting full-service health professionals, like pediatric nurse practitioners, dentists, and optometrists into programs and schools serving disadvantaged students is also necessary to close any achievement gap between black and white students.

The school systems themselves are not entirely to blame, according to Rothstein. He says that schools are segregated today because neighborhoods are segregated. He thinks that residential integration will beget school integration, which will then raise the achievement of low-income black children. Unfortunately, he says, federal requirements that communities must pursue residential integration have not been enforced, and federal programs designed to move low-income families into middle-class communities have not been effective.

In summary, Rothstein thinks that schools continue to be segregated and that, until neighborhoods are desegregated, schools won't be desegregated again.

Other Solutions

Martha Minow, the Jeremiah Smith, Jr. Professor of Law at Harvard Law School, and the school's dean, wrote a book called *In Brown's Wake: Legacies of America's Educational Landmark*, which was published in 2010. Working from the premise that schools across the country are more segregated than ever, she set out to find

ANOTHER LEGACY

More and more experts are cautioning that schools in the United States are becoming segregated again. Racism is still a major issue in this country as of 2016. Yet there is more to Thurgood Marshall's legacy than his legal victories. He broke into the law's ultimate "old boys' club" when he became a Supreme Court justice in 1967. And because he broke the color barrier, he blazed a path for future minorities.

After Marshall's retirement in 1991, Clarence Thomas became the second African American to serve on the Supreme Court. So far, he and Marshall are the only two. However, women and other minorities are now represented on the bench, too. Sandra Day O'Connor became the first female justice, appointed by President Ronald Reagan in 1981. President Bill Clinton appointed Ruth Bader Ginsburg to the bench in 1993. President Barack Obama placed two females on the court, Sonia Sotomayor, who is also the first Latina or Hispanic Supreme Court justice in our country's history, and Elena Kagan. In a case of history coming full circle, not only did Kagan clerk for Thurgood Marshall shortly after graduating from Harvard Law School, but she also became the first woman to serve as solicitor general of the United States.

The justices of the United States Supreme Court in 2010 were a diverse group.

Martha Minow, dean of Harvard University Law School, presented the 2013
W. E. B. Du Bois Medal to Justice Sonia Sotomayor.

out why and to answer the question of whether the Brown ruling's original promise has been unfulfilled.

Minow says that she gives *Brown* its due for abolishing Jim Crow laws and legal racism in America. She feels that there was real progress made toward racial desegregation of schools, even if just for a short time, and expresses disappointment that the federal court and administrators stopped focusing on the enforcement of desegregation orders in the early 1970s. She writes that "racial integration has largely receded from public priorities when it comes to K-12 public schools."

However, she admits that the impact of *Brown* still resonates in colleges and universities, workplaces, and media depictions. She also points out that the case has had positive effects on advocacy for gender equality, policies for disabled students, and the concept of school choice, which ironically started as a policy implemented by those who were trying to avoid court-ordered desegregation.

Minow also addresses what some people call *Brown*'s "great and central failure." The United States is a legally desegregated society because of the court's decision, but it did not bring about a dramatic change in the culture, as some people had hoped. It didn't produce much integration outside of the schools. She says that while people of different races live and work and study side by side, there doesn't seem to be a shared feeling of mutual respect, engagement, and investment.

Minow explains that people have actually done research to try to understand why school integration didn't bring about closer connections between the races. One book, written just before 1954, argued casual contact usually is not enough to overcome prejudices. That requires "sustained contact among people of equal status who participate in cooperative activities"—which was in short supply for many years after *Brown*. Minow says that social science researchers have documented the benefits of mixing people of different backgrounds in school and work settings, which include higher academic achievement, reduced prejudices, the ability to see others' perspectives, and an increased capacity to think of creative solutions to problems. However, she does not know how to achieve this, especially since the law can change practices but not necessarily attitudes—as *Brown* once proved.

Agreeing with Graglia and Rothstein that modern school segregation is mostly caused by community segregation, Minow proposes that charter schools could be a solution.

Charter schools are like public schools in that they're free, but families can choose which charter school they want their child to attend. Charter schools are often designed to best serve the needs of particular students in a particular community. Some focus on the basics, the traditional school subjects with which some students struggle, while others specialize in certain areas of academics, such as science and math. Some have special arts or music programs. There are charters that cater to students who need day care for their children, and charters that work with children who want to go to college. The main goal of charter schools is to make sure every child has access to a quality education, which is exactly what Thurgood Marshall was trying to accomplish with *Brown v. Board of Education*.

Minow feels that charter schools, which accept students by public lottery, can help to vanquish residential segregation and attract students from different neighborhoods—although she points out there is also a risk that charters will encourage self-separation by race or ethnicity, too.

Marshall's Legacy

Today, it's fair to say that the nation's schools are no longer truly desegregated, yet the case of *Brown v. Board of Education* accomplished a lot that still holds true today. First, it brought about a deeper understanding of how pervasive and ugly racism is, and how the government was wrong in supporting it. Those who lived through segregation describe it as "a massive, sustained, nationwide assault on the spirits of black people to disable us from being able agents of our own lives." *Brown* helped to abolish the racial caste system that existed in the United States after the Civil War.

It has also kept alive many debates about how to best educate children from different areas and different cultures, as well as the question of how best to fund schools and educational programs. Roger Wilkins, a professor of history and American culture at George Mason University, elaborated on this in 2004:

> In this country what we do right now is we give the best resources and the best teachers to the places where the kids come to school and have the greatest amount of social capital. And we give the worst resources and the least able teachers to the kids who need it most.
>
> So if we're going to change what is occurring in this society, you don't take away resources from the kids who are doing well in good schools. What you do is you increase very substantially the resources and the talent level of the teachers in the schools that are not doing well ...
>
> I don't think that Thurgood Marshall and his associates, most of whom I knew personally, believed that a black child had to sit next to a white child in order to get a good education. They understood that the resources followed white kids. So if a black kid was going to get a good education, you had to have integration.

John McWhorter, a professor of linguistics at the University of California, Berkeley, once commented, "The problem with education now is not that *Brown* didn't work. It's that we have other kinds of cultural problems besides segregation and the overt racism that we had at that time."

America is now a country of rapidly growing and changing levels of diversity. Society is no longer just about the dynamic between whites and African Americans. The United States has a population that includes Latinos, Asians, Native Americans, and Europeans. Refugees and immigrants continue to enter the country every day. The country has gone back to some level of segregation in schools, not deliberately in defiance of *Brown v. Board of Education*, but due to greater societal forces. It may take more work and more years and more people committed to integration to make it truly happen, but the ruling in *Brown v. Board of Education* will continue to ensure that all of the people who make their home in this country will get an education.

Sheryll Cashin, a professor at Georgetown University Law Center and author of *The Failures of Integration: How Race and Class Are Undermining the American Dream*, commented in 2004:

> I think that we need a model of integration that's a 21st century multicultural model, not one where blacks bear the burden of assimilating into white America, but more [one where] white people assume the responsibility of becoming comfortable living in a society where they're going to be surrounded by very different people, different races, and getting comfortable with that.

Perhaps Thurgood Marshall himself said it best in 1992, less than a year before his death:

> The legal system can force open doors, and sometimes, even knock down walls. But it cannot build bridges. That job belongs to you and me. We can run from each other, but we cannot escape each other. We will only attain freedom if we learn to appreciate what is different and muster the courage to discover what is fundamentally the same. Take a chance, won't you? Knock down the fences that divide. Tear apart the walls that imprison. Reach out: freedom lies just on the other side.

An official portrait of Supreme Court Justice Thurgood Marshall

CHRONOLOGY

1908 Thurgood Marshall is born in Baltimore, Maryland. He is the second son of Willie and Norma Marshall.

1914 Marshall enters first grade at a segregated Baltimore elementary school.

1921 Marshall attends high school at the segregated Colored High and Training School.

1925 Marshall enters college at Lincoln University, an all African-American school, in Pennsylvania.

1929 Marshall marries his Lincoln classmate Vivian "Buster" Burey.

1930 Marshall graduates from Lincoln with honors, applies to law school at the University of Maryland, and is rejected because of his race. He then applies to Howard University School of Law and is accepted.

1933 Marshall graduates first in his class from Howard University School of Law.

1935 Marshall sues the University of Maryland for refusing to admit Donald Murray, an African-American student, to its law school. He wins the lawsuit a year later.

1936 Marshall and Vivian move from Baltimore to New York City when he takes a job with the NAACP.

1938 Marshall becomes chief legal counsel for the NAACP.

1946 Marshall is honored with the Spingarn Medal from the NAACP.

1952 Marshall begins to argue *Brown v. Board of Education* before the Supreme Court.

1954 The Supreme Court decides in Marshall's favor, and school segregation is legally abolished in America. Soon after this decision, Marshall's wife, Vivian, dies of cancer. Marshall remarries, to an NAACP employee named Cecilia Suyat.

1956 Marshall's first son, Thurgood Junior, is born.

1958 Marshall's second son, John, is born.

1962 Marshall becomes a federal appeals court judge.

1965 Marshall is appointed US solicitor general by President Lyndon B Johnson. He is the first African American to hold the position.

1967 Marshall becomes the first African-American Supreme Court justice in American history.

1991 Marshall retires from the Supreme Court for health reasons.

1993 Marshall dies from heart failure at the age of eighty-four.

GLOSSARY

affirmative action The practice of improving the educational and job opportunities of members of groups that have not been treated fairly in the past because of their race, sex, etc.

alienate To make unfriendly, hostile, or indifferent, especially where attachment formerly existed.

ally Person, group, or nation associated or united with another in a common purpose.

alma mater The school, college, or university that someone attended.

apartheid Racial segregation, especially the former policy of segregation and political and economic discrimination against non-European groups in the Republic of South Africa.

appeal A legal proceeding by which a case is brought before a higher court for review of the decision of a lower court.

boycott To refuse to buy, use, or participate in something as a way of protesting; to stop using the goods or services of a company or country until changes are made.

busing The act of bringing children by buses to a school that is far from the area where they live so that the school will have many children of different races.

compulsory Required by a law or rule.

correspondence courses A class in which students receive lessons and assignments in the mail and then return completed assignments in order to receive a grade.

covenant A formal written agreement between two or more people, businesses, or countries.

cultured Having or showing good education, tastes, and manners.

disbar To take away the right of a lawyer to work in the legal profession.

dissent To publicly disagree with an official opinion, decision, or set of beliefs.

etiquette Rules indicating the proper way to behave.

grilling Questioning intensely.

grueling Very difficult; requiring great effort.

Harlem Renaissance A blossoming of African-American culture, particularly in the creative arts, and the most influential movement in African-American literary history, from approximately 1918 to 1937.

hiatus A period of time when something is stopped.

intervene To become involved in something in order to have an influence on what happens.

Jim Crow laws Any of the laws that enforced racial segregation in the South between the end of Reconstruction in 1877 and the beginning of the civil rights movement in the 1950s.

jurisdiction An area within which a particular system of laws is used.

lynch To kill someone illegally as punishment for a crime.

massive resistance A strategy used by Virginian representatives to prevent desegregation following *Brown v. Board of Education.*

mentor Someone who teaches or gives help and advice to a less experienced and often younger person.

mongrel A pejorative term for those born of mixed-race parents.

nullify To make legally void; to make of no value or consequence.

pawn To deposit something with another as security for a loan.

plaintiff A person who sues another person or accuses another person of a crime in a court of law.

posthumous Happening, done, or published after someone's death.

precocious Exhibiting mature qualities at an unusually early age.

rapport A friendly relationship.

recuse To remove oneself from participation to avoid conflicts of interest.

stipulate To demand or require something as part of an agreement.

unanimous Agreed to by everyone.

union An organization of workers formed to protect the rights and interests of its members.

SOURCES

CHAPTER ONE

pg. 15: Haugen, Brenda. *Thurgood Marshall: Civil Rights Lawyer and Supreme Court Justice.* Minneapolis, MN: Compass Point Books, 2007, pp. 50–51.

pg. 23: Mara, Wil. *Thurgood Marshall: Champion for Civil Rights.* New York: Scholastic, Inc., 2004, p. 10.

CHAPTER TWO

pg. 29: Hitzeroth, Deborah and Sharon Leon. *The Importance of Thurgood Marshall.* San Diego, CA: Lucent Books, 1997, p. 16.

pg. 30: Haugen, p. 25.

pg. 32: Zelden, Charles L. *Thurgood Marshall: Race, Rights, and the Struggle for a More Perfect Union.* New York: Routledge, 2013, p.17.

pg. 42: Haugen, p. 81.

CHAPTER THREE

pg. 46: National Association for the Advancement of Colored People. "NAACP History: Charles Hamilton Houston." http://www.naacp.org/pages/naacp-history-charles-hamilton-houston.

pg. 50: National Association for the Advancement of Colored People, "Our Mission." http://www.naacp.org/pages/our-mission.

pg. 50: The NAACP Legal Defense and Educational Fund. "Our Mission." http://www.naacpldf.org/about-ldf.

pg. 51: Howard University School of Law: Brown @50, Fulfilling the Promise. "Oliver White Hill." http://www.brownat50.org/brownbios/BioOliverHill.html.

pg. 54: The National Museum of American History. "Separate is Not Equal: Brown v. Board of Education. The Court's Decision." http://americanhistory.si.edu/brown/history/5-decision/courts-decision.html.

pg. 55: Biography.com. "Earl Warren Biography." http://www.biography.com/people/earl-warren-9524239.

pg. 56: Greenhouse, Linda. "William Brennan, 91, Dies; Gave Court Liberal Vision." *New York Times*, July 25, 1997. http://www.nytimes.com/1997/07/25/us/william-brennan-91-dies-gave-court-liberal-vision.html?pagewanted=all.

pg. 56-57: *Ibid.*

CHAPTER FOUR

pg. 62: NAACP Legal Campaign. "Murray v. Maryland." November 11, 2008. http://naacplc.blogspot.com/2008/11/murray-v-maryland.html.

pg. 63: PBS.org. "Jim Crow Stories: Smith v. Allwright." http://www.pbs.org/wnet/jimcrow/stories_events_smith.html.

pg. 64-65: PBS.org. "Jim Crow Stories: Morgan v. Virginia." http://www.pbs.org/wnet/jimcrow/stories_events_morgan.html.

pg. 66: Shay, Alison. "On This Day: Shelley v. Kraemer." Publishing the Long Civil Rights Movement, May 3, 2012. https://lcrm. lib.unc.edu/blog/index.php/2012/05/03/on-this-day-shelley-v-kraemer/.

pg. 71: Mara, p. 59.

pg. 74: Hitzeroth, p. 60.

pg. 76: Somervill, Barbara. *Journey to Freedom: Brown v. Board of Education*. Mankato, MN: The Child's World, 2010, p. 19.

pg. 76: CivilRights.org. "Brown v. Board of Education." http://www.civilrights.org/education/brown/.

pg. 77: Haugen, p. 69.

CHAPTER FIVE

pg. 81: Altschull, Herb. "Brown vs. Board of Education: Here's What Happened in 1954 Courtroom." *Los Angeles Times*, May 18, 2014. http://www.latimes.com/nation/nationnow/la-na-nn-brown-v-board-ap-original 20140518 story.html.

pg. 81: *Ibid.*

pg. 81: *Ibid.*

pg. 81: *Ibid.*

pg. 82: Hitzeroth, pp. 63, 65.

pg. 82: *Ibid.*

pg. 83: *Ibid.*

pg. 87: Somervill, p. 20.

pg. 87: Library of Congress. "Brown v. Board at Fifty: 'With an Even Hand.' The Aftermath." https://www.loc.gov/exhibits/brown/brown-aftermath.html.

pg. 87: PBS.org. "The Supreme Court: Landmark Cases: Cooper v. Aaron." http://www.pbs.org/wnet/supremecourt/democracy/landmark_cooper.html.

pg. 90: *Ibid*.

pg. 90: The National Center for Public Policy Research. "Brown v. Board of Education, 349 U.S. 294 (1955) (USSC+)." https://www.nationalcenter.org/cc0725.htm.

pg. 93: Hitzeroth, p. 69.

CHAPTER SIX

pg. 98: Brownstein, Ronald. "How Brown v. Board of Education Changed—and Didn't Change—American Education." *Atlantic*, April 25, 2014. http://www.theatlantic.com/education/archive/2014/04/two-milestones-in-education/361222.

pg. 98: Greenspan, Jesse. "History in the Headlines: 10 Things You Should Know About Brown v. Board of Education." History.com, May 16, 2014. http://www.history.com/news/10-things-you-should-know-about-brown-v-board-of-education.

pg. 100: Columbia Law School. "Brown vs. Board: Opposing Views." https://www.law.columbia.edu/focusareas/brownvboard/bvbopposing.

pg. 100: *Ibid*.

pg. 101: *Ibid*.

pg. 101: Garland, Sarah. "Was 'Brown v. Board' a Failure?" *Atlantic*, December 5, 2012. http://www.theatlantic.com/national/archive/2012/12/was-brown-v-board-a-failure/265939.

pg. 102: Rothstein, Richard. "Brown v. Board at 60: Why Have We Been So Disappointed? What Have We Learned?" Economic Policy Institute, April 17, 2014. http://www.epi.org/publication/brown-at-60-why-have-we-been-so-disappointed-what-have-we-learned.

pg. 107: Goldberg, Jesse. "The Surprising Consequences of Brown v. Board of Ed." *Atlantic*, December 1, 2010. http://www.theatlantic.com/national/archive/2010/12/the-surprising-consequences-of-brown-v-board-of-ed/66820.

pg. 107: *Ibid.*

pg. 108-109: PBS.org. "Brown v. Board of Education 50 Years Later." May 17, 2004. http://www.pbs.org/newshour/bb/law-jan-june04-brown_5-17.

pg. 109: *Ibid.*

pg. 109: *Ibid.*

pg. 110: *Ibid.*

pg. 110: Hitzeroth, p. 99.

FURTHER INFORMATION

BOOKS

Aldred, Lisa. *Thurgood Marshall: Supreme Court Justice*. Black Americans of Achievement. New York: Chelsea House, 2004.

Haygood, Wil. *Showdown: Thurgood Marshall and the Supreme Court Nomination that Changed America*. New York: Knopf, 2015.

Rollyson, Carl, and Lisa Paddock. *Thurgood Marshall: Perseverance for Justice*. Bloomington, IN: iUniverse, 2012.

Starks, Glen L. and F. Erik Brooks. *Thurgood Marshall: A Biography*. Westport, CT: Greenwood, 2013.

Zelden, Charles L. *Thurgood Marshall: Race, Rights, and the Struggle for a More Perfect Union*. Routledge Historical Americans. New York: Routledge, 2013.

WEBSITES

Biography: Thurgood Marshall
www.biography.com/people/thurgood-marshall-9400241

In addition to summarizing the basic facts of his life and career, this site allows visitors to get to know Thurgood Marshall through numerous videos.

Thurgood Marshall

www.history.com/topics/black-history/thurgood-marshall

This site provides a variety of articles, videos, speeches, and links that help to illustrate the life of Thurgood Marshall.

Thurgood Marshall: Associate Justice, United States Supreme Court

www.arlingtoncemetery.net/tmarsh.htm

Read Marshall's lengthy, informative obituary from the *New York Times* at this site.

ORGANIZATIONS

The Thurgood Marshall Center for Service and Heritage
1816 12th Street, NW
Washington, DC 20009
www.thurgoodmarshallcenter.org

BIBLIOGRAPHY

Adler, David A. *Heroes for Civil Rights*. New York: Holiday House, 2008.

Bolden, Tonya. *Portraits of African-American Heroes*. New York: Dutton, 2003.

Good, Diane L. *Brown v. Board of Education*. Cornerstones of Freedom. New York: Children's Press, 2004.

Haugen, Brenda. *Thurgood Marshall: Civil Rights Lawyer and Supreme Court Justice*. Minneapolis, MN: Compass Point Books, 2007.

Hitzeroth, Deborah and Sharon Leon. *The Importance of Thurgood Marshall*. San Diego, CA: Lucent Books, 1997.

Kent, Deborah. *Thurgood Marshall and the Supreme Court*. Cornerstones of Freedom. New York: Children's Press, 1997.

Mara, Wil. *Thurgood Marshall: Champion for Civil Rights*. New York: Scholastic, 2004.

Rowh, Mark. *Thurgood Marshall: Civil Rights Attorney and Supreme Court Justice*. Berkley Heights, NJ: Enslow Publishers, 2002.

Somervill, Barbara A. *Journey to Freedom: Brown v. Board of Education*. Mankato, MN: The Child's World, 2010.

Zelden, Charles L. *Thurgood Marshall: Race, Rights, and the Struggle for a More Perfect Union*. New York: Routledge, 2013.

INDEX

Page numbers in **boldface** arc illustrations. Entries in **boldface** are glossary terms.

affirmative action, 24–25, 56
alienate, 82
ally, 21, 57
alma mater, 33
Alston v. School Board of Norfolk, Virginia, 49
American Opportunity Act, 23–24
apartheid, 93
appeal, 62–63, 73, 85, 90, 95

Baltimore, 10, 15, 28–29, 35, 37, 64, 85, 87
Black, Hugo, 51, 53, **54**, 55, 57
boycott, 15, 19–20, 83
Brennan, William, 53, 56–57
Bridges, Ruby, **84**, 85
Brown, Linda, **58**, 74, 94
Brown v. Board of Education of Topeka, Kansas, 6–7, 16, **17**, **18**, 19, 38, **39**, 40, 46, 49–50, 53–54, **54**, 56, 59, 63, 67, 70–77, 79–85, 90, 92–94, 97–98, **99**, 100–103, 107–110

Burey, Vivian "Buster," 33, 35, 38, 40, 80
busing, 101

Calloway, Cab, 34, **34**
charter schools, 108
Civil Rights Act of 1964, 21, 42, 79, 100
Clark, Kenneth, 72, 74, 86
compulsory, 76, 101
Constitution, US, 5–6, 12, 30, 52–53, 55–57, 63, 66, 81, 90, 93, 101
Cooper v. Aaron, 87, 90
correspondence courses, 86
covenant, 66
cultured, 28

Davis, John, 74–75, 80
disbar, 38
dissent, 55–57, 94
Douglas, William O., 53, **54**, 57

Eisenhower, Dwight, 19, 53, 87
etiquette, 6

Fourteenth Amendment, 30–31, 52, 62, 66–67, 71, 73, 75–76, 93

Great Migration, 12
grilling, 24
grueling, 42

Harlan, John Marshall, II, 53, 55–56
Harlem Renaissance, 12, 34, 38
hiatus, 75
Hill, Oliver, 48–49, 51, **51**
Houston, Charles Hamilton, 14–15, 35, **36**, 37–38, **44**, 45–49, 57, 59, 62, 71, 73, 80
Howard University, 14, 35, 46–48
Hughes, Langston, 32–34, **34**

intervene, 19, 90

Jim Crow laws, 6, 11–12, 35, 45–47, 59, 64, 76, 107
Johnson, Lyndon B., 7, 21, **22**, 23–24, 40, 42, 48, 95
jurisdiction, 30, 48

Kagan, Elena, 47, 104, **105**
Kennedy, John F., 21, 24, 40, 48, 90, 95
Kennedy, Robert F., 21, 90
King, Martin Luther, Jr., 20–21
Ku Klux Klan, 10–11, **11**, 28, 42, 55

Legal Defense and Educational Fund (LDF), 20, 38, 49–50, 67, 70, 90–91
Lincoln University, 31–35
Little Rock Nine, 19, 86–87, **88–89**, 93
lynch, 10–11, 50, 79

Malcolm X, 20
Mason-Dixon Line, 10
massive resistance, 16, 83
McCree, Wade Hampton, Jr., 48, **49**
McLaurin v. Oklahoma State Regents for Higher Education, 67, **68–69**
mentor, 14, 35, 45, 57, 59, 80
Meredith, James, 90–91, **91**
Mills v. Board of Education of Anne Arundel County, 15

mongrel, 6
Morgan v. Virginia, 64–65
Murray v. Maryland, 60, **61**, 62

NAACP, 14–15, 20, 37–38, 40, 46–50, 64–65, 71, 73–74, 76–77, 81, 86, 92, 95
Nabrit, James M., Jr., **17**, 73
nullify, 81

Obama, Barack, 79, **96**, 98, 104

Patton v. Mississippi, 65
pawn, 32
plaintiff, 67, 73, 94
Plessy v. Ferguson, 6, 10, 12, 30–31, 37–38, 46, 53, 55, 62, 67, 74, 76
posthumous, 47
precocious, 28

rapport, 37
recuse, 38
Regents of the University of California v. Bakke, 25
riots, 10, 12, 14, 24, 50, 85, 90
Roe v. Wade, 24, 57

Second Circuit Court of Appeals, 21, 40, 48
"separate but equal," 6, 10, 12, 31, 47, 53–54, 71, 73–75, 80
Shelley v. Kraemer, 65–66
Smith v. Allwright, 63–64
solicitor general, 21–22, 40, 42, 48, **49**, 104
Southern Manifesto, 82
Spingarn Medal, 38, 47
stipulate, 30
Suyat, Cecilia "Cissy," 40, **41**

unanimous, 19, 23, 53, 66, 76, 95
union, 33, 47
University of Maryland, 14, 35, 60, 62

Vietnam War, 23
Voting Rights Act, 23, 42

Warren, Earl, 51, 53–55, **54**, 56, 75–76
White Citizens' Council, 81, 85

ABOUT THE AUTHOR

Rebecca Carey Rohan has written several books for Cavendish Square Publishing. She lives in suburban Buffalo, New York, with two children and several rescued pets.